A Latvian Tale
of Love, War
and Peace.

Anna's
story

Anna Lejiņa

Edited and translated by Atis Lejiņš

Rīga, 2011

ISBN: 1456567993
ISBN-13: 9781456567996
Library of Congress Control Number: 2011901272

Anna's story: key words

Latvia, Rīga, Baltic States, Russian Empire, Revolution, First World War, Russian Civil War, Second World War, Soviet Union, Nazi Germany, bombing of Dresden, refugees, British Zone of Occupation in Germany, Australia, America, Christian missionaries in India, Afghanistan.

Table of Contents

Preface

By Atis Lejiņš

Anna's Story is a vivid memoir about a young Latvian girl who blossoms into a loving wife and mother against the backdrop of the momentous events of the first half of the Twentieth Century.

In simple but poignant language she uses her remarkable memory to show us how people lived, worked, struggled, loved and came to terms with death and tragedy in a Europe ripped apart by revolutions and two great wars. Events take us from the revolution of 1905 in Latvia, then part of Imperial Russia, to 1945 in the British zone of occupation in northern Germany.

We see the fall of the Russian empire, the rise of communism, the birth of the new state of Latvia and its destruction by two tyrants, Hitler and Stalin. Anna then recounts how she and her young family flee west to seek safety with the American and British invading forces. Fate saves them from terrible death in Dresden where thousands of refugees perished in the fire-bombing of that city at the close of the Second World War. More people died from the bombing of Dresden than from the atomic bomb being dropped on Hiroshima, if the deaths caused by radiation are not included.

But Anna does not judge. She simply tells us her story and from it we marvel at how love triumphs over death. Perhaps her story can inspire hope in the younger generation who are facing a new century with daunting challenges and threats. The 21st Century may not turn out to be much different than the 20th Century. As the ancient Greeks discovered, though the form may change, history basically repeats itself.

Anna's youngest son, Atis Lejiņš, through many phone calls and letters from Stockholm to Los Angeles, convinced her to write down her story before her death in 1984, just six weeks short of her 80th birthday. The Latvian version of Anna's story *Dzīvot dzīvu dzīvi* (To live a full life) was published in Sweden in 1986, then in the re-born Latvia in 2002.

Included in the text are several pages written by Anna's husband, Eduards Lejiņš, describing his wartime experiences fighting in four different armies during the Russian Civil War. He died in 1989 at age 95 just as Latvia was awakening from the long nightmare of Soviet occupation and, together with Estonia and Lithuania, was ready to bring down the Soviet Union through the most effective weapon of all – non-violence. In August 1989 instead of throwing bombs, the people joined hands in a human chain linking the three capital cities of Tallinn, Rīga, and Vilnius and sang their way to freedom. This is what the history books now call *The Baltic Way*. In the concluding chapter Anna's son, Atis tells how he returned to Latvia and how Latvian independence was finally regained.

Together with her beloved husband, Eduards, Anna now rests in peace in the Lejiņš family plot not far from where the family farm, *Viesturi* was in Jelgava, Latvia.

I am indebted to Susan Tosch for her painstaking work in editing my English translation and for her many valuable suggestions and sound advice in helping me to bring *Anna's Story* to the English reading public.

Introduction

By Susan Tosch, writer and artist

I have to put my hand up right from the start. I've never been to Latvia and before I read *Anna's Story* I had no interest in learning about my cultural heritage. That door was well and truly locked and I saw no point in trying to open it. Why bother, I thought. It's so hard to find out anything about Latvia, except about the war and God knows I've heard enough about that to last me a lifetime. I know that sounds awful but the whole concept of war repulses me. To tear families apart and force people to run for their lives when they have done nothing wrong just seems so barbaric to me. In my mind there are no circumstances where that level of physical and psychological violence should be inflicted onto people, particularly innocent ladies and their much loved babies. I find it unbearable to think that my sweet, gentle grandmother and so many other women like her had no choice but to pick up their babies and run for their lives. And to think of my own mother, as a little girl suffering such terror, makes me put my hands over my ears and start singing "La, La, La," as loud as I can. Not a very mature way to deal with life's realities I know.

My first memory of Anna Lejiņa and her family was when a parcel arrived from overseas to our home in Australia. It was the Christmas of 1974 and I was 9 years old. Included in the parcel was a piece of Latvian amber for me. At the time I didn't understand why these people I had never met thought it was so important to send me such a strange gift, a little honey-coloured stone.

I knew my mother was Latvian and that when she was a child the whole world had gone to war. She and her family, fearing for their lives, fled their homeland and at first sought refuge in Germany and later, in Australia but that was pretty much all I knew. Almost every question I had ever asked my mother about Latvia ended with either, "I was too young to remember" or "I don't know what happened after the war".

My father is an Australian, of Scottish descent, and like many men of his generation had no idea what he was getting into when he married a woman from a different nationality. About the same time I received my little honey-coloured stone, my mother started to teach me how to speak Latvian but when my father found out he flew into a rage. Maybe he felt threatened that he would be locked out of our conversations? Instead he locked the door on my Latvian heritage and I never dared mention Latvia in front of him again. So I grew up knowing my mother was Latvian but it had nothing to do with me. I was Australian.

Then in 2008 I met up with Anna's son, Atis Lejiņš. He helped me find the courage to unlock that door my father had forbidden me to open - to see the Latvia behind the horror and suffering, the Latvia beyond the war. The real Latvia, the beautiful Latvia, the Latvia my mother should have grown up in.

When Atis offered me the opportunity to help bring *Anna's Story* to an English speaking audience I jumped at the chance. There must be others like me, I thought, Latvian descendants scattered all over the world who for whatever reason do not have the Latvian language, the key to opening the door to their ancestral past.

I've learned language can be a powerful tool but it can also be used as a weapon, it can both open and close doors. Anna understood the power of language. Already able to speak several languages, at the end of her schooling she searched for direction in her life. She considered becoming a doctor and then a missionary in India but in the end chose to become an English teacher, hoping it would give her an opportunity to see the world. She could never have imagined how that decision would alter the course of her life.

The further into her story I read, the more I began to see similarities between Anna and the women in my own family. As I began to get to know her strengths and weaknesses I had a surprising revelation. I was like Anna! I was Latvian! Until then I thought it was only my mother who was a "true" Latvian, not me.

So, will I ever get to experience Latvia for myself? I don't know the answer to that but I do know I don't have to stand on her soil or experience her magical, mystical beauty to know I belong to her. Now I carry her in my heart and I can stand tall and say - I am a Latvian - and I will never let anyone take that away from me again.

Chapter 1.

Life under the tsars: war and revolution

The Irbe family

I was born in the summer of 1904 in Vidzeme, Plāņu county, district of Valka, in Sarkaņskola, Latvia, which was then part of the Russian tsarist empire. It was there that my father, Kristaps Irbe, hailing from Courland, and my mother, Paulīne Jostsone[1] from Vidzeme, settled down after marrying shortly before the preceding century merged into our's. Father was a schoolteacher, and I was already the fourth child in the family. The first, Paulis, died when he was still a small infant; the second, Vitauts, was already three years old and fate had decided that he would die in a slave labor camp in the Siberian gulag in 1942. The third, Tālivaldis, or Tālis for short, was two years old but he was to live only another six years. Two years after me the family grew with Paulis, named in honor of our deceased brother, followed by Jānis, and then my little sister Skaidrīte, the very youngest, who was born only one year before the First World War. She was born in Vitebsk, Belarus, where we had moved to and died in the Australian desert on her family's orchard irrigated by the Murray River in the late 1970's.

My father Kristaps was born in 1874, in Sātiņu county, Tukums district in Courland in the very place where his father, Fricis was born in 1842, only a few years before Krišjānis Valdemārs caused a sensation

---

1   Some Latvian surnames are spelt differently depending if the person is male or female. For example: Jostsons is used for males, Jostsone is used for females. Lejiņš is used for males, Lejiņa for females. The male form of the surname, Lejiņš is pronounced – Leyinsh. The female form of the surname, Lejiņa is pronounced – Leyinya. The letter " j " is pronounced " y ". For example: Silvija is pronounced Silviya. The letters ā, ē, ī, ū can have a diacritic placed above them to indicate a long vowel sound. The letters č š ž ģ ķ ļ ņ can have a diacritic placed above or below them to indicate a softening of their sound.

at the Tartu university that went down in Latvian history - he had the audacity and courage to write next to his name on the dormitory door the word, *Latvian*. It was the beginning of the long birth of the Latvian nation. Until then only Germans, unlike the masses of Latvian peasants and craftsmen, were considered capable of higher learning. The few educated Latvians immediately passed into the ruling upper German caste, upon finishing university.

Fricis Irbe was quite well off because he owned half a manor, which he had received from the local German baron. While hunting hares the baron had accidentally shot Fricis in the eye and as compensation for the loss of his eye he granted Fricis some land from his enormous holdings with a building on it for farming activities. This enabled my grandfather to educate his five children, and also to assist his brother Kārlis to finish his theological studies. Kārlis Irbe eventually became the first bishop in free Latvia. He was the one who, in the ancient church ledgers kept by the local German priests since the Christianization of the Latvian people in the 13th century, traced the Irbe family roots back to the 16th century. The Irbe clan's heroism in the battles of the Latvian tribes against the invading German Teutonic Order, who brought Christianity with the sword, was noted in the ledgers. The bishop's wife was very elegant, probably German.

We hardly knew them. The bishop once paid a visit to his benefactor brother Fricis, who by then lived in the Zaķu village, across the Venta River, with his son, Žanis. I was at the railway station among those waiting to receive him. He chose me as his support to lean on, as he hobbled somewhat. To me he seemed a big heavy man and I tried not to stagger.

The second time I saw him was in the Rīga cathedral, when he ordained new ministers to the cloth. The third time was when we all followed his coffin to its final resting place in the Forest Cemetery in Rīga.

Grandfather Fricis was an average sized man with dark blue eyes and dark hair and was somewhat slow by nature. His wife, Jūle was the same. In the summer all the relatives with their innumerable children visited them. What a grand time we had! There was no end to the merriment and mischief!

After his wife's death, my grandfather went to live with his housemaid Lavīze, on his daughter Anete's and her husband Ernests Kalniņš' rented farm, *Zemītes,* near Kandava, who had twelve children. Fricis and Lavīze were quartered in a cottage in the big garden. How tall and full were the chestnut trees there! And when they blossomed the whole garden was filled with large white blossoms that looked like candles. Lavīze loved to talk a lot, so we called her Chatterbox. I liked her, but I became uncomfortable when she let loose with her juicy, farm hand's rough language. But my brothers listened to her in ecstasy.

Lavīze was present when grandfather died. This is what she told us:

One morning Fricis remained in bed sleeping. I brought him his breakfast and went back to the kitchen. Then I heard him shout. I looked and saw he was completely awake, but weak and pale in the face. He shouted, 'Lavīze, look through the window. Look! See, Jūle is waving to me with her hand… I'm coming, darling, I'm coming!' And so your father followed his wife to the after life.

Lavīze wept. Now she was left all alone.

Fricis died in 1929 in a Latvia free and independent and completely different from that in which he was born. Only grand manors testified that once the Baltic German gentry ruled the country, but now Latvian school children attended school in these grand buildings. Jānis Jostsons, my other grandfather on my mother's side, died in 1943, aged 93 years, in the third year of the German occupation of Latvia. He had five children; a son, who died when only 20 years old of pneumonia and four others, all girls, who were well educated. Jānis was well-off since he managed a dairy, run by the local baron. One of his daughters, my mother Paulīne, was born in 1880 in Rencēnu county, Valmiera district. When she was a child, she became friends with the baron's daughter Elza. Everything Elza learned about running the household, my mother also learned. This enabled her in later years to become a teacher of housekeeping at the Ventspils secondary school.

Grandfather Jānis was a fine specimen of a man; good-looking, blond, blue- eyed, strong. He became angry if things didn't go right. He was a very industrious, God-fearing man and he respected the landed gentry. He was still only a kid when Latvians were allowed to start owning land. Grandmother and grandfather both finished their schooling at the local parish school. She wrote poems; at her funeral we sang songs she had composed.

My grandmother was a stout, rather short woman, with dark hair. She had a merry outlook on life and was a great storyteller, just like me, only I had blond hair and grey-blue eyes. When she acted the 'witch', she laughed in the most devilish manner. With her mouth wide open she stuffed a big potato inside which she had carved to look like horrid wide spaced teeth. We kids hid under the beds on the double even though we knew it was only 'Grandma'. Better to be safe than sorry! After her death in 1920, just when the newly proclaimed Latvian state had managed to drive out all foreign forces, Grandfather Jānis came to live with us in Ventspils.

Sarkaņskola

My father was Sarkaņskola's headmaster as well as a teacher. Our living quarters were at one end of the school building on the bottom floor and included; a large guest room, a large bedroom, and a large dining room with a big table in the middle of the room. Everything seemed big to me. I was already one year old, in 1905 when in Latvia, the tillers of the soil, the working classes, and the educated classes rose up against the masters; the German barons and the Russian administration. I remember being in my mother's lap sitting at the dining room table. The white lamp was in the middle of the table. My grandmother came in and positioned herself by the door. Two soldiers followed her in with rifles with fixed bayonets in their hands. Years later, when I related this to my mother, she was amazed that such a small child, only one year old, could remember this. I can still see it all, even to this day, as if I was looking at a painting. Perhaps as a tiny creature I instinctively felt my mother's fear, when the soldiers came in to look for my father. He had escaped by jumping out the window.

I was two years old, and can remember only that I lay on the floor, kicking and screaming like mad. I never wanted to go to sleep in the middle of the day. Grandmother said, 'Look, how capricious that little girl is. Daughter, if you don't give her a good hiding now, the child will suffer a difficult life with such a stubborn streak.'

My mother then thrashed me with a birch switch but the more she thrashed me, the louder I screamed. When the first droplets of blood appeared on my bottom, my mother got a fright. I was put in bed and I dropped off to sleep immediately. I didn't speak for two days and Mother cried that she had trashed the voice out of me. Since then, after any big argument, I was in the habit of keeping silent for two days.

When my little brother Jānis was born, his cradle was hung in the bedroom. It was my job to swing him when he cried. When the crying seemed to last too long, I swung the cradle with such determination that with every push, little Jānis flew up in the air. The crying usually ended then and the baby fell asleep.

On one side of the garden was the well with its sweep and bucket. It was strictly forbidden for us children to approach the well and look down it, because the 'Old man of the well' could yank us down into hell.

Unfortunately, Paulis was in the habit of doing what he pleased. When he was about three or four, he took to throwing pebbles into the well and then would watch to see what happened to them. Beyond the garden, in the corner of the county house, my grandmother usually sat and knitted while glancing, every now and then at the well. Suddenly she heard sounds as if they were coming from the very bowels of the earth. Running up to the well, she saw that Paulis was thrashing about in the water, blowing bubbles out of his mouth!

'Help! Help! Paulis is in the well!' Grandmother screamed.

Luckily there was a choir rehearsal at the school, and Father along with the whole choir was at the well in no time. My mother tore down the path with her arms full of bed sheets. A slim young man put one leg in the bucket and while clutching the rope attached to the sweep, was lowered, standing upright, into the well. Paulis was pulled out. The men laid Paulis in the middle of the sheet and held both ends while they threw him about from one side to the other. Paulis came to life!

The second accident with Paulis was as follows: The horse was harnessed to the carriage in front of the veranda. Our parents were getting ready to ride to the Remembrance of the Deceased Day at Smiltene cemetery. We kids were looking forward to the outing! I grabbed Jānis and put him next to me, holding him tight. Paulis climbed up at the end of the carriage. Suddenly the horse bucked and pulled the carriage forward. Paulis fell and hit his head against the wheel. He stood up with his head bleeding. I screamed in an awful voice. Mother came running, and we saw a white patch in the middle of his skull. He was taken to the hospital in Smiltene.

After a couple of weeks Mother journeyed to Smiltene to fetch Paulis but he was nowhere to be found in the hospital. Mother ran in the direction of the forest and caught up with a gypsy girl who had Paulis with her. She refused to give Paulis back to Mother. She claimed he was her boy, black hair and blue eyes. Finally both women agreed that for a sum of three rubles Mother could have Paulis back. Later, whenever Paulis got into trouble, Mother complained, 'Paulis! Paulis! What have you done!

And I had to pay three rubles to get you back!' That was a month's wages for a housemaid.

Father earned his keep in money and kind. He was given land to use and farm animals. My biggest fear was of the gander. He ran after people and when he caught them, he beat them with his strong wings. Once I hid the hen that Mother had decided to put on the table. I dearly loved all peaceful animals.

At the other end of the garden was the barn. I used to sit there with Tālivaldis and discuss 'things'. He knew everything. I regarded him as an 'oracle'. Once I asked him what my future held.

'Tālis, little brother, if papa could build the tallest of ladders, do you think I could reach heaven?' Tālivaldis 'The Great' now gravely replied, 'You are a woman, you wouldn't understand.'

Mother once told me that she had been worried about me because I often sat as a small child in one place and gazed at the sky. In our house however, prayers were said only in the evening, before going to bed, when we children repeated two lines, 'To bed now we must go. Father, please now close our eyes.'

My older brother, Vitauts never played with us. He was forever going fishing. We were allowed to play by the river only when father took a nap in the grass on its banks and then took a swim. We kids pulled irises out of the riverside mud and formed live beings from them. The brown tops became cows, the 'candles' became sheep etc. Jānis just sat and looked on, and we came to call him the 'landlord'. I was his 'wife', Paulis was the 'servant' and Tālivaldis was the 'baron'.

Father threw us into the whirlpool and then right away yanked us out. I certainly didn't like being under the water but poor Mother lived in constant fear that something bad would happen to us. Entering the bog was strictly forbidden, still we were drawn to it, because there was a place there where, when you ran over the brown peat, the ground swayed. If father found out we had been there, we invariably got a hiding, and after that we had to kiss his hand in forgiveness. The thrashing didn't hurt at all, because father didn't thrash us in anger.

So thus I lived my life, hopping up and down, with my head full of ideas, and my father teaching me to dance. He maintained that dancing cultivated the personality. Without me nothing could take place! However, things did not always go so smoothly for me. One day Mother took me to Smiltene to visit her friend who owned a sweets factory. Sweets were a rare treat for us kids. Glancing around the room I noticed that on the long tables *gosniņas*[2] lay in long rows, waiting to be wrapped into the little pieces of colored paper. They were still somewhat soft. I moved myself to the other end of one of the long tables. Mother and her friend appeared to be looking at a book. I grabbed a gosniņa and hid it in my black stocking above my knee. Then I pinched another one and put it in my other stocking. The lady treated us to tea and cakes. Oh my! My *gosniņas* began to melt down my legs! From fear of being discovered the cake no longer tasted like it should. I kept jerking my mother by the sleeve to let her know I wanted to go home. As a parting present the lady gave us a big paper bag full of sweets to take home. I nearly died of shame!

Winter. Snow drifts and sledges. What joy! Tālivaldis, rushed down the hill on his sledge, but fell into an ice-hole in the river. Vitauts pulled him out but the next day he had to be taken to the hospital. Only on a late spring day did he return home and was put in a comfortable bed. Oh, those eyes! Joy and tears overwhelmed us as we all wept. Even writing these lines today I have to cry – I can still see his eyes. He couldn't speak. He could only move one arm and his neck somewhat. Mother could read his thoughts from his eyes. He could swallow food. I ran, day in and day out, telling my beloved brother about everything that went on in the outside world.

---

2 *Gosniņas* (with soft 'n') is the dimunitive plural of cow – *govs* in Latvian. Singular gosniņa. Nowadays, despite the avalanche of imported sweets, *gosniņas,* though suffering a major set-back, are still manufactured in Latvia, but under another dimunitive plural form *gotiņas.*

The time came for harvesting the summer's rye. Behind the veranda's leafy trees the rye was cut and tied into bundles. Suddenly Tālivaldis began to throw his good arm about. His eyes wanted to tell me something but couldn't, and tears started to fall down his cheeks.

I jumped out the window, as it was closer than the door, and raced to Mother screaming, 'Tālis is dying! Tālis is dying!' Mother held his hand and wept. Father caressed her forehead. Then Tālivaldis sighed and departed for eternity.

My dear brother was put in a white coffin and placed in the guestroom. The priest spoke, the guests sang, and I kept pulling Mother's hand. I pleaded to be lifted up so I could see my beloved brother. Someone did lift me up. I grabbed the coffin's edge and would not let go. Somebody finally got me down. I began to cry and scream that I wanted to see my brother. A woman grabbed me and pulled me out of the room. I wasn't taken to the cemetery and I ran after the carriages shouting that I should be allowed to go. I wanted to die so I could be with my dear Tālis in heaven. His death was a fateful blow to our family.

My forever restless, thrifty mother who constantly kept everything clean and dressed her children in becoming clothes, overworked herself. Father applied for an easier job in Vitebsk, not far from Latvia, in the Belarus part of Imperial Russia as a headmaster in a Latvian colony school. Thus I was taken away from my motherland to a foreign land, away from my beautiful world.

We stood on the platform and waited. The train! It was the first time I had seen one. I was already in my sixth year. How terrible it looked and how terrible it huffed! I was afraid, nevertheless I liked it. I felt grown up because, you see, I was traveling on a train to Russia. As soon as we got inside, I flattened my face on the window pane – trees, fields, houses – all ran quickly past my eyes. I was swiftly carried away from my beautiful world.

Later, when I was ten years old, we paid a visit to grandmother and grandfather Jostsons, who lived not far from Sarkaņskola. I ran off immediately to see the old school. Nothing seemed so big anymore in that lonely place. Life's pulse had ceased there. The school mistress invited me in and served me pancakes. We sat in the same room with the same lamp – but instead of my big family being there it was just the two of us. I said goodbye and ran away as if I was running from a graveyard, past the small bog, through the forest. When I saw somebody coming, I hid behind some bushes. Soon I was back at Grandmother's cottage, sitting on the foot-bridge and observing the little fishes playing.

Vitebsk

Our big river, the Daugava, which the Russians called, the Dvina, ran by Vitebsk. A long bridge had been built over it and not far from the river, on Nizhnigorodskaya Street, there was the Latvian school. Next to it stood the Lutheran church with lilac trees planted alongside the street on the inside of the church's white fence, and flowers on the outside. In front of the school there was a large square for games and exercises on the parallel bars. Further on, in a remote place, was the outhouse. At the end of the street was the Jewish quarter. There you had the Jewish boys with whom the gentile kids used to 'wage war' against.

The school was big. The sleeping quarters for the boys were in the cellar, while for the girls they were in the attic. In the big class room you had four classes with only two teachers. Each teacher taught two classes at the same time. The third teacher taught two older classes in a third, smaller room.

I was seven years old and sat in the first class. I didn't listen to the teacher because I didn't like her. On the other hand, I delighted in listening to my father when he came to the class to tell us a story from the Old Testament. Once, the teacher told me to read some story aloud. I 'read' and peeked at the same time to see what the others were doing. Hence I failed to notice that my father was standing behind me and had observed my 'reading'. He asked the teacher to let me read the next story. I said I wouldn't since it had not been assigned. The fact was that I didn't know how to read, hence couldn't read it. I understood letters by their visual form and I knew how to write them down but I didn't know how to name them and put them into words. Usually I knew the stories off by heart, because a helpful school mate before class read them aloud several times. Now Father had made this discovery he took me to his room, sat me on his writing table, put a book in front of me, and started to teach me how to read. I was very glad, because now I would be able to read all the stories myself. There was only one problem – I didn't want to learn anything off by heart anymore, except piano pieces.

The teacher couldn't stand Paulis. She pushed him in the corner and grabbed him by his ears and his hair. I told Paulis, 'If she pushes you around again, drop immediately to the floor and start rolling about and foaming at the mouth.' I demonstrated how it should be done. The next time Paulis actually did that. From that time on the teacher left him alone or asked him to leave the class room.

Jānis was very active with a head full of white hair. He was forever darting in and out among the school kids. He was everybody's favorite. One day when he was running about he banged his head against a pan, which a pupil had lifted from the stove and the hot sauce ran down his neck.

Mischievous deeds: Usually my brothers and I played together with Milda and Aleksis, whose father looked after the church and school. Aleksis constantly had a runny nose. I hated that, but since he did as I said, I didn't reject him. The Jew behind our square had stacks of wood, logs, and planks for construction. A big pear tree grew in front of his window. He jealously guarded his building materials. We kids, on the other hand, couldn't wait until the pears were ripe. We quickly scaled the fence. Aleksis stood guard by the cottage. Paulis and Milda were to pick up the pears from the ground, while I climbed up the tree. I picked the pears and shoved them into my wide blouse which was pulled tight

11

with a rubber band. I was halfway down when the pears started to drop out from the waistline of my blouse. Suddenly Aleksis arrived with the news that the door had squeaked! My assistants flew away and I was left to slide down the tree alone, bruising my hands and legs. And that was not the only time, when they deserted me! Luckily the old man had not seen us and we hid the pears under our pillows and gnawed them at night. We soon came to the realization that they would have to be eaten after they had ripened.

The Jew's yard kept attracting me. It was like a big town! When he wasn't home, we played there, though without making too much noise. Everything had to be carried out secretly. In our game Jānis was always the 'banker', Paulis was the 'tramp', 'drunkard' or 'thief', nicknamed the 'Raven', because of his black hair. I was 'Catherine the Great', Vitauts was 'Nūnītis' (crybaby), because he quickly lost his nerve and started to cry. Skaidrīte, my younger sister, when she was old enough to play games, got the sobriquet 'Skunk'. Why? I can't remember. Milda and Aleksis played their parts as various assistants. The 'banker' as a rule never worked but when he was given sweets, he divided them honestly among all of us and never forgot Kristīna, the school's housemaid. She was Russian and had learned to speak Latvian quite well. Kristīna then would clap her hands together in joy and lift Jānis high up in the air.

I was the leader and one day decided that I was not afraid to climb the log pile all the way to the top. I did reach the top, but coming down, as I slid on my bottom, one log at the very bottom broke loose and rolled over me. Father carefully laid me in bed and the doctor examined all the discs of my backbone.

'Well, little lady, this time you were lucky,' the doctor concluded. But I did spend three months lying on my back in bed.

Once in the dark I had hidden under the stairs which led to the girls' sleeping quarters. In the morning the girls came down the stairs and went through the dining room and into the kitchen to have their breakfast by the stove. I waited under the stairs for a girl to climb down. I jumped out from my hideaway and grabbed her. The girl, taking fright, whacked me on the head with the pan she was carrying, so hard that I almost lost consciousness!

I loved to exercise on the parallel bars, especially on the higher ones. Swinging high up, I released my grip momentarily and then quickly grabbed the bar again. Once I missed and landed on my back. I tried to regain my breath. I'm dying! I can't breathe! I rolled onto my knees with my head down, quickly made the sign of the Cross, and said goodbye to Mother. I regained my breath.

In the school there was one thieving boy, dirty and lazy, who was often beaten with the belt. One day he convinced Jānis and Paulis that they should empty the pockets of the coats belonging to the members of the choir. The coats were in the staircase room. If they did it, he promised to give them sweets. They did! After that Father thrashed Paulis and Mother thrashed Jānis, but I tried to stop the hiding in every way possible. Mother even dropped her glasses on the floor, and they broke. After supper, during evening activities I became too loud. The teacher ordered me to stand in the corner but I refused. I shouted that I would denounce her to my father and ran out of the class. Father only laughed. He took me on his lap.

'From now on, you do as the teacher says. Alright?' he said sternly.

'Yes,' I replied, and, indeed, henceforth I did.

Mother sometimes let me sleep upstairs in the girls' quarters. That's where Kristīna also slept. We all loved her. When the girls began telling ghost stories, I crept under Kristīna's blanket. One evening I decided to be a spook myself in the girls' quarters but not in the room where Kristīna slept. The beds were positioned end to end, and thus in the middle of the room there was a sort of gangway. I covered myself in a white sheet and extended my arms in both directions. The moon came out and shone straight at me. Suddenly I felt as if a 'real' ghost had crept up behind my back!

'Help! Help!' I screamed. The girls had a good laugh.

Once our new male teacher, having had one too many drinks, climbed upstairs to the girls' quarters and, from outside the door sang, for example, 'Kristīna, my very first girl. Don't break my heart now... Please let me in!' Silence. Then, 'Goodnight, fair damsels!' followed by the sound of his receding steps.

When thinking about Kristīna I see an icon of Mary with baby Jesus in her arms, in the corner next to Kristīna's bed. At Easter she always took us kids, me, Jānis and Paulis, to the Russian church to celebrate Mass. That was a wonderful experience for us all. There was always something new. Around midnight, the likeness of Christ was carried around the church. The church bells rang through the whole town. Everything was so beautiful! When the procession returned to the church, where there were no seats, everybody fell to their knees and kissed the floor or else touched their foreheads to it. The priests walked in front of the altar swinging incense jars and singing, 'Christ has risen,' and the congregation echoed, 'Truly he has.' Then followed the refrain, 'God, have mercy!' It felt like I was already in heaven.

Then it was time for the celebrations. Everybody got up and started kissing one another. Kristīna kissed the youngest and best looking lad in no uncertain fashion even though she was no longer that young anymore. Easter was the most beautiful holiday for all of us. Once Mother was walking along a street on Easter morning and a slim priest with a long, red beard grabbed her and kissed her plumb on the lips. From that time on she was never caught on the streets again on Easter morning.

The Latvian Lutheran church seemed dreary to me. My only activity there was to help Vitauts treadle the pedals of the organ. Father played the organ at the Latvian church services. I don't know why I felt like that. Perhaps because the Latvian church in reality, was not Latvian. It was a German institution, which the Latvians had copied lock, stock, and barrel, instead of adapting it to the Latvian spirit, song, and world outlook. The Latvian peasant had to listen for many centuries to the sermons of the German priests admonishing him to obey the barons, and then they chained the more rebellious ones and put them in the pillory, right in front of the church where they were whipped before the service began. That is the heritage of the Latvian church. How can one feel free, uplifted and joyous in such a church?

One year we also visited Uncle Kārlis and Aunty Milda in Latvia. And then we were off, out into the countryside and into the forest! Two strong horses were harnessed to each cart. The lake. Swimming galore. After that the afternoon snack was served; *runshtiki* (small round pieces of white bread), cranberry jam and milk. The adults drank stronger beverages. Oh! How good everything tasted! My beloved pine forest, how fragrant it was in the hot sun! How I hated the gadflies, which bore into the skin of my precious horses, who constantly had to lift their legs up and down and shake their heads.

We picked strawberries for Aunty Milda. My cousins were amazed that I didn't eat them. Once I had overeaten strawberries and became sick. That's why I didn't as much as put one of them in my mouth. One of my cousins, Olģerts, found that out. The boys threw me on the ground and held my arms and legs while one of them stuffed strawberries into my mouth, one after the other. It's a wonder I didn't choke or suffocate. After that, I assumed a very martial attitude toward my cousins - but I began to eat strawberries again! So in fun and games, the summer went by too quickly.

Once I also visited the Russian capital city, St. Petersburg. Aunty Mice (pronounced Mit-se), my father's sister, came to visit us in Vitebsk and I was allowed to travel with her back to St. Petersburg. She didn't have children and said that I should stay with her for a while. Her Russian husband was a station master at a railway station in a forest not far from the city. I loved to accompany him to the station and observe how the trains rushed past us without even stopping. He spoiled me. I often got small presents from him. When Aunty went hunting with him they took two white dogs with black spots.

Their old maid demanded that after each meal I should say thank you. I just couldn't do that. I loved sunflower seed. My uncle said that he would not give me any more *siemechkas* if I didn't say thank you. He ate them right in front of my eyes. Then I started practicing saying, thank you, thank you, thank you. On the third day after finishing the meal, I jumped up and managed to utter 'thank you' – and then I bolted for the door. Uncle bought a whole pound of sunflower seeds and I stuffed myself until I was almost sick.

When aunty Mice traveled into St. Petersburg to buy new furniture I was allowed to accompany her. Leaving the train, I was frightened by the big city. We also visited Aunty Anna, my mother's sister. She had fled from her home to St. Petersburg because she had become fed up with doing the farm's chores, especially soaking the harvested flax in water, a heavy job. I begged to be left with her and finally got my way.

Aunty Anna was the chief nurse in a psychiatric hospital. All the personnel lived in one three-storied building, and all the floors were exactly the same. Aunty had only one room but it was a very beautiful one. Once, I watched from the window, down at the kids playing outside, and I summoned enough courage to start walking down the stairs to join them. But the downward climb seemed to take too long and I began to retrace my steps. I got lost and began to cry.

'Why are you crying, little dove?' the Russian women asked but I cried all the more. Luckily Aunty Anna appeared and I was happy once again, though I didn't try to climb down the stairs on my own anymore.

One day I was taken to the movies. On the screen I saw a beautiful garden with a beautiful maiden. Suddenly a rider on horseback charged up to the fence, leaned over, seized the maiden and galloped off. Only one of her shoes remained laying in the grass. Her grief-stricken father with his hair turned grey overnight went off into the wide world in search of her. After the show, Auntie's boyfriend came to meet us, and bought us all kinds of sweets, and we went home to Auntie's to enjoy them. I performed a dance, playing the part of an actress, but unfortunately I tripped and fell over. Auntie's friend wanted to pick me up, but I claimed that in this dance you were supposed to fall down. We spent a lovely evening together until Aunty whispered to me, 'This guy is polishing everything off and we will have nothing left.'

In the morning Aunty was hurriedly summoned to the hospital because she was the only one who could calm down the patients. I tried to endear myself to her in all manner of ways. I polished her shoes with a black ointment I found in a nice little box and was surprised to find that the shoes didn't shine afterwards. Aunty arrived. Gales of laughter! That wasn't the shoe polish! Oh, I loved her!

Later Aunty Anna became the first 'famous Anna'. During the war she volunteered as a nurse at the front. One night, after a battle, several doctors and field nurses were playing cards to relax, but Anna kept on caring for the wounded men. It was said to be an awful scene, to see the soldiers suffering, dirty and bespattered with blood. It was a dark night and it was raining. Suddenly Anna sensed that somebody was standing behind her. She was washing a wounded soldier's legs, whose nails had grown into the flesh and had begun to fester. Quickly she spun around – and there, standing in front of her, was a stately grey-haired general!

'Where are the others?' he demanded. He requested she go with him. He was the Grand Duke, brother of Nicholas the Tsar! He strode through the mud in the dark, and Anna, stumbling and half running, tried to keep up with him. In a Russian peasant's cottage the Grand Duke pinned the highest award for nurses to her breast – a gold medal!

The army retreated. Panic! Anna ran. She jumped over a ditch and cut her leg. A young officer, galloping along the dirt road on horseback saw her fall. He jumped off his horse, quickly bound her bleeding knee with his silk scarf, lifted her up onto his horse, and they galloped off. Later they married.

After living in St. Petersburg for some time, Aunty Mice arrived to tell me that the stork had brought me a sister, Skaidrīte. Did I still want to stay? I was sorry to leave, but I needed to see my little sister right away.

I went back home and looked after my sister. Friends arrived with cakes and sweets, and father treated us three, Jānis, Paulis and me, to the movies. Usually we sat in the front row with our heads craned back as much as possible and looked at the screen. This was supposed to be the best place. We got it into our heads that the others further back couldn't see as good as we could. If somebody was shot in the film, I tried to figure out how much the film's owners would have to pay the parents of the actor in compensation.

'Beat the Jews!' somebody suddenly screamed in Russian in a most horrid voice. The light bulbs were smashed, chairs went flying in all directions, and we were the first to shoot out the door.

But Latvian society in Vitebsk was blossoming. Father became the main leader. There was the choir, concerts, and theatre shows. Mother performed songs solo. She was beautiful, slim and elegant. She wasn't 'loud', instead one felt an atmosphere of mystery about her. When the war had already started I entered the tsarinas Marijas gymnasium preparatory class, where I began studying French.

War: 1914-1918

When father was mobilized into the Russian army I was freed from paying the full tuition fee. Together with the Jewish girls, I had to attend school in the afternoon from three until eight in the evening. Since father was an ordinary soldier, Mother on that account received a small allowance as the wife of a soldier. This was enough only to pay for the reduced tuition fee. I came from a poor family, but the Jewish girls had to attend evening school like myself because of their religion. Many Latvian men were mobilized at the beginning of the war, and my father probably served in the 20th 'Latvian' division, so called because it consisted mainly of Latvian men. They sang their ancient Latvian war songs and marched in high spirits in East Prussia toward Koenigsberg because the tsar promised them a quick victory.

After the first successes against the Germans, Father, dressed in the Russian army's long coat, got leave and paid us a visit. He looked grand! His long whiskers had been trimmed short. He kissed me, threw me up in the air, and pulled my long braid. And then he began to tell tales from the front! Father, with his friend Dzenis, had decided it wasn't worth dying for the tsar. Accordingly in the very first battle they fell facedown in a potato field and there they remained until their unit was stopped and came running back over the field in full retreat. In other battles – well, it depended on the situation – sometimes they charged forward in the heat of the summer's dust and shouted, 'Charge!' He didn't visit us a second time. When father and Dzenis returned to the front, they disappeared without a trace. While the Russian generals argued amongst themselves, the Latvian men bled in the land of the Old Prussians, which had been conquered by the Teutonic Order in the 13th century. The German supreme commander, Paul von Hindenburg, crushed the Russian army near Tannenberg, at exactly the same place where in 1410 the Lithuanian Grand Duke Vitautas, together with the Polish King Jagailis, defeated the Teutonic order when it was preparing to invade Lithuania.

It was said that some 30,000 Latvian men either died or were taken prisoner in the battles in Eastern Prussia. The German army poured into Lithuania and was soon able to occupy Courland, when we were amazed by the news that the tsar had given permission to form national

Latvian riflemen units in the Russian army! Our boys knew no bounds in their enthusiasm!

At school, I made friends with Natasha, and on occasion while going home, we turned into the small cathedral which was located in the very centre of the big, cobble-stoned square. Natasha used to kiss the feet of the wax statue of Christ and was amazed that I didn't do it. I explained that the feet were dirty and I didn't want to expose myself to dangerous germs. I also added, that it wasn't Christ at all but only an image made by a human being. Natasha stared at me in amazement, but never raised the subject again.

Once Natasha's father gave me a book about Christ with beautiful pictures in it. I hid myself in one of the cathedral's niches and read it all in one go. I wept and cried, 'What cruelty! How could the Father allow his son to be nailed to the Cross!' This was a completely different God from the good, warmhearted little Latvian God. But I loved Jesus and promised not to forget Him.

I often dreamed about Jesus, but I remember only one dream. I saw narrow stairs, which lead to heaven. Below was a huge crowd of people. One naked man, dressed only in a loin cloth, chased us about and beat us with a towel. Those hit were not allowed to climb up the stairs. He wanted to hit me at all cost, but in the end failed. After this dream I started to help all the town's old women, including the Jews, only the women, not the old men because I was somewhat scared of them. They seemed so rough. For example, I helped to carry their heavy loads and so forth. I forbade the boys to cheat an old, half-blind Jewish woman on the street corner by putting in her hand old money, no longer in currency, for sunflower seeds.

Strolling with Natasha along the street to the cathedral and back, I tried not to look too hard at the smart handsome lieutenants and senior class gymnasium students, who also took their promenades along the same street, to the bridge and back. When the tsar himself and his daughter

Tatyana came to visit Vitebsk we girls from the gymnasium stood in a long line on the square and shouted 'Hurrah!' for all we were worth when they passed by.

In winter, when it was dark coming home from school, I shortened the trip by putting my school books inside an old, hard-covered notebook and then tied them together with a belt. I placed my bottom on it and rode down the steep embankment and onto the frozen Daugava River. This way I halved the distance, since from the other side of the river there was only a bit to go to reach our home. I was often joined by Minna a Jewish girl, who lived right on the bank with her grandparents. Unfortunately riding on the book 'sleigh' caused the heels of my boots to wear out more quickly, because I needed to brake the speed of my ride.

Occasionally I earned a few rubles by playing dance pieces on the piano in the school's big hall whenever there was an event. Vitauts was the cloak-room attendant and I had to bang the piano keys very hard so that the dancers could hear me. The next day my fingers hurt.

Revolution

Revolution! The tsar had been overthrown![3] Some people were scared, others happy. Lessons in school were often interrupted. In our Latvian school the big hall was full of refugees from Latvia. The Germans were at the very gates of Rīga, but our heroic Latvian Rifles had stopped them. The refugees gave me a lot of work. I wrote confidential love letters for the girls and boys on a contractual basis. I translated them in Latvian from Russian novels. The lovers paid me in kind.

The Russian soldiers in the school's back yard often brewed a tasty buckwheat porridge. We kids also got our share. People said that these

---

3   The tsarist government was overthrown in 1917 in the so called February revolution. The tsar abdicated from the throne on March 15.

were good times. Latvian patriots were happy that now for once Latvia would become free. Russia, however, didn't remain free[4] long.

The shops began to suffer food shortages. Sometimes you had to stand in long lines from ten in the evening until dawn before you got through the door. My brothers, Jānis and Paulis, had to sleep on the street under one blanket in front of the shop. When the shooting began, they took to their heels and charged home through the door breathless. Jānis cried because while he was running he had lost one of his galoshes.

When fires broke out in the town, we needed to see them at any price. My brothers held me by my legs, (a superb safety precaution, indeed!) while I climbed out the attic window and up onto the roof. I gripped the roof's tin joints and like a cat crept to the chimney. From there I could see everything and wonder which fine house was now going up in flames. If only they didn't torch my girlfriend Klupte's house!

Getting down was much harder. I tied a rope that I had taken with me around my waist and let the other end drop down to my brothers below. This way I had more courage to let myself down from the roof and place my feet on the window-sill. Mother couldn't stop wondering how I could recount with such enthusiasm and in so much detail the fires that raged in different parts of the town.

One day, skipping on the bridge on my way to school I ran into a stately young lieutenant with a trim black moustache, 'gold' buttons on his uniform, a sword at his side, and spurs that faintly chimed as he walked. Suddenly a powerful arm from behind, knocked me to the side – I spun around to see a soldier, who bellowed at the officer, 'Bastard! You didn't greet me!' The lieutenant immediately shot his hand to his cap in greeting, but it was too late. The soldier tore off his epaulettes, the 'gold' buttons, and then spat in his face. Laughing with his girlfriend

---

4 The communist *coup d'etat* against the Russian democratic Provisional Goverment , otherwise known as the October Revolution, took place six months later on November 7. Russian democracy lasted six months.

he proudly continued on his way. The officer wiped his face with a white handkerchief and threw it into the Daugava River. I cried – how awful!

Another time, when our Latvian boys and girls scout troupe was marching along the street, the militia stopped us and tore off the insignia from our leader with the order to disband this 'bourgeois army'. The Reds were strengthening their positions in Vitebsk.

Later, however, I had a falling out with our scout leader. One morning I was tardy getting ready and he called to me from the door, 'Anna dearie, hurry along. That's a good girl!' I was still struggling with my long hair, sitting in front of the mirror. He was a good-looking boy and in love with our Girl Scout leader. He stood behind me and through the mirror I saw his smiling face as he caressed my hair and said, 'Little Anna, your hair shines like gold!' I blushed. I was thirteen years old. Was he my first love?

The refugees in our school were moved to another place, and our family moved into two other smaller rooms next to the kitchen because typhus victims were quartered in our school. Mother got some kind of a fever, Jānis and Paulis contracted dysentery, Vitauts came down with pneumonia, while Skaidrīte succumbed to stomach typhus. Her back was covered with awful boils. I helped the doctor's assistant when he changed the bandages. Likewise I carried out the night pot to the outhouse for my brothers and washed it clean with chlorine or green soap and changed the linen for the whole family. I fetched soup every day from the Women's Salvation Corps. When everybody was fed I ran off to school. If only the school's director didn't find out that there were typhus patients in our lodgings! I would be thrown out of school! When a typhus patient died, his clothes and mattress were burned in the exercising yard. Shooting continued on the streets, and here and there fires continued to burn in the city. Usually pupils and students were sent home one hour earlier.

Skaidrīte was close to dying. The doctor's assistant scribbled something on a piece of paper and ordered me to fetch the medicine without delay. But there were long lines at the pharmacy – I had to wait. I started to cry, and explained that my little sister was already turning cold. I got the medicine immediately. I ran back home, falling and tripping in the snow and rain. After a while rosy spots appeared on Skaidrīte's face. 'She will live, little girl, she will come through it!' the doctor's assistant assured me. And she truly did recuperate. However, even though she was already four years old, after the sickness I had to teach her how to walk again. Finally the whole family got well and I could once again hop about on one foot!

Soon another calamity fell upon us. My school stopped giving fee allowances for the needy. My friend, little Klupte, who was Jewish, organized a lottery so that I could pay for the full tuition fee. Her father even donated a new lamp to attract buyers. The money came in, but by that time the school's administration had changed its mind and had reinstated the allowance. When we finished our class we bought the teacher flowers with the lottery money and Minna, my other classmate, bought a small box of chocolates for the school's head mistress.

I had been in trouble with the headmistress earlier over something I did at school. We were not allowed to run up and down the stairs that lead from our class room on the ground floor, to the second class room on the first floor. One pupil did that once, but when running past the headmistress's door, she suddenly yanked the door open and shouted that the miscreant should be so kind as to step into her room. But the miscreant vanished so fast, that only a long flying hair braid was seen going past. That was me. I had bet that I wouldn't be afraid to do it. The problem was that only three girls in both classes had long braids – I, Natasha, and one girl from the other class. The headmistress interrogated us no end, put us in a line, and made us whirl around as fast as we could. I didn't confess, because I was afraid I would be expelled from school. But the other two girls didn't betray me either. Then, when the headmistress received a present from us, she was elated and closed our 'case'.

Uncle Kārlis Irbe, the church dean, established a shelter for Latvian refugee children in another province. He visited us and took Paulis and Jānis with him when he left. My mother cried, but my brothers remained silent, apparently they didn't understand what was going on. After they left, two Latvian girls from the Latvian colony in Vitebsk came to live with us. They were high school students and paid us in kind for their keep. This was how we got lard, flour and honey. They had to sleep in the dining room behind the curtain in one bed; Mother was by the other wall with the small table for washing in the corner. Vitauts slept on the floor in the room by the piano, and I slept on a small couch which, when I turned around, lost its leg and I landed on the floor.

Mother sewed until three in the morning for her private customers. Then I got up, together with one of the students, Milda, to go and stand in line until nine when the shop opened. Her father had been killed in action, probably in East Prussia, and usually we were the first to arrive. We fought mightily to stop our eye lids from clamping shut. Mother no longer trusted Vitauts, because once when returning home from the shop carrying a loaf of corn bread he ate the whole lot. In winter we were so bundled up in clothes we were hardly able to get up off the ground when we slipped and fell on the icy footpath. On the other hand, these mishaps provoked peals of laughter that brightened our souls.

After the visit to the shop we went to the market where the peasants had arrived from the countryside and we strolled from one cart to the next. They usually poured a little milk in a cup to taste, to prove the milk was fresh. When we had enough to drink we went over to the vegetable and apple carts. While I gossiped with the seller, Milda pinched some produce and deftly put it in her wicker basket. On such occasions I forgot about Christ.

Behind me in the gymnasium sat Minna, a Jewish girl. She was rather pretty, blond, with blue eyes but had dirty unkept hair and her nose was forever running. On occasion you could see lice crawling in her hair. The school's governess, with whom one had to speak French, completely ignored her. She simply walked passed her as if she was invisible. But Minna was my shadow in whatever I did! One day, I decided to take her home with me. Minna was beside herself with joy. I pleaded with Mother to sew a new school dress for her and rub *zabodil* vinegar in her hair. After that a kerchief was tied tightly on her head so that the lice would die once and for all. Mother reminded Minna to take the kerchief off only the next morning and then thoroughly wash and rinse her hair.

Minna lived with her grandparents in a Russian village next to the Daugava River where they had a goods store and where they also traded items under-the-counter. From them we got everything Mother ordered. This was how we escaped famine even though there were often food shortages. After we had tidied up Minna we received sugar and thread, and at school Minna shared her chocolate with me which we finished off on the spot.

Minna looked beautiful now; she was no longer her former self. Her grandparents were so happy that they invited me to the Jewish Easter Passover. My 'friends' warned me not to go, because I would have my Christian blood sucked out of me. But I went.

The dining room was in the cellar and smelled of garlic. On the table was a huge, seven forked candlestick holder and a big heap of *matzah* bread. The grandfather, with something that looked like a box on his head, covered me with a striped cloth and murmured prayers. We three, Minna and I, and the grandmother, sat in silence. It was an eerie feeling! Then the old woman shuffled to her feet and handed us broth which we gulped down with the *matzah* bread. I loved *matzah!*

One day I heard a knock at the door. I opened it and who did I see? From where had they turned up? Just standing and not saying a word! I embraced both my brothers, Paulis and Jānis, and kissed the poor darlings. Only then did they open their mouths. They had run away from the shelter, because they wanted to be with their Mother! Paulis had barely turned eleven, and Jānis was only ten years old! Soldiers had pulled them in through the train window and bundled them out again the same way on the Vitebsk railroad platform. Now Mother had two more mouths to feed.

In the summer of 1918 Mother gave us, her children, to the local Latvian colonists as shepherds. Their houses were made according to the Latvian custom with thick thatched straw roofs, a dense apple orchard, bee hives, a granary and a barn. The road leading to the farm was planted with trees on both sides. The harvest was good. The Russians, from the local village demanded bread - was there anyone who dared not give it to them? Mother worked as a servant and seamstress but Skaidrīte, the smallest of us, was the little princess, spoilt by everyone. We had to get up at four in the morning, but I was exempted from milking the cows, since I just couldn't learn how to do it. Every morning I prayed to God that he could take five years of my life if I could sleep just a little longer! My bare feet froze in the dew, and when it got hot the tall grass and underbrush cut my legs when the cows ran away and I had to drive them back. Life was not easy for a little shepherd ...

On Saturday evenings I went with the farmer's daughter, Paulīna, who was twenty-two years old, either to the *Vecherinka* dances in the Russian village or the *Frankusezi* balls that the Latvians held. Oh how I wanted to dance! Now and then luck did smile upon me. Once a Russian boy, about 17 or 18 years old, in a bright red shirt and long boots bowed awkwardly in front of me and asked me to dance the Polish dance, the *Krakovyaka*. We Latvian kids used to sing in Russian, 'The German, Russian and Pole went to dance the *Krakovyaka* – German, German, how foolish you look. You cannot dance the *Krakovyaka!*' What luck! He jumped up and clicked his heels together, but I, the 'lady', had to run in small steps to one side, then the other, according to the beat. With the Latvians, adults danced with adults and I didn't like to dance with small boys because they didn't know how to dance properly.

One fine day, while I was herding the cows, I reflected on the psyche of these animals – just like human beings. Some were good natured, others troublemakers, and some thieves. Take my favorite cow! She obediently chomped the green grass growing alongside the planted rye field, which had just sprouted green and juicy. She didn't pluck one stem of this forbidden fruit! But as soon as I turned my head I saw with one eye how she quickly snatched the tempting rye! When I turned my head back, she was back placidly pulling at the grass, in all innocence, on the very edge of the field.

Suddenly I saw a man coming along the sandy road. He looked rather unusual, with a long, well-cut beard. I drove the cows closer to the road. He asked me, which way it was to our home, to the farmer's house, where we were staying. I couldn't utter a word - I just waved my hand pointing in the direction. 'Thank you,' he said and went off. I observed him until he turned off the road and continued along the lane that led to the house.

Oh! Could he be my father? But he had been missing already for four years! The sun was setting as I hurriedly drove the cows home. Jānis, Paulis and Skaidrīte, from the other side of the river had also seen him and were now quickly driving their cows along with me. I ran up to the house and through the window saw my father embracing my mother, who was wiping her tears away with her apron. I darted into the room and waited ...

Father told his story. The remainder of his unit had retreated from East Prussia through Lithuania and had come quite close to the Latvian border, where he and his buddy Dzenis were put in a signal service building, which was destroyed by a bomb. Father received a blow to his head and remained lying on the ground unconscious for a good while. When he awoke, Dzenis said that bullets were flying from all sides, and both took to their heels, braving the crossfire, and headed to the nearby woods. Having run deep into the forest they found a crossroads where there was a resting place, a pub and a stable for horses. The pub's owner, a Jew, came out to meet them and eyed their Russian army uniforms. Father explained that they were really Latvians and needed to rest a little. When it was dark they would continue their journey to Latvia. The proprietor told them to go upstairs to the hayloft to sleep.

Both exhausted soldiers had hardly slept a wink when German soldiers woke them and ordered them to climb down. Father's buddy was a big strong fellow and understood immediately what had happened. He grabbed the pub owner by the throat and would have choked him to death if the German soldiers had not pulled him away. So, there, both of them became German prisoners of war. While they were sleeping the proprietor had run six kilometers to the closest village occupied by the Germans to inform them that two 'Russian' soldiers were at his pub.

In the prison camp in Germany Father's job was to stir a saccharin mixture in a big pot. Living off only potato peels and saccharin his eyesight gradually worsened and it looked as if he would lose his sight completely. He fainted while standing by the cauldron and almost fell into its boiling mixture. He was put into hospital where he became acquainted with a German army officer of high standing, and since father knew German, the officer invited him to go to Latvia to help him organize the schools under the German occupation. By now the Germans had driven out the Russian army from all of Latvia and the Germans ruled the land.[5]

This officer, upon my father's word that he would return to Latvia, gave permission for him to travel to Russia to fetch his wife and children. But upon arrival in Vitebsk, father's friends who held high posts in the newly established Soviet government invited him, Kristaps Irbe, to stay and assist them in their work. Soon Latvia would be free both from the Germans and the Russians. They promised to find a good job for father. At that time, Latvians had a lot of power in Russia. My father had to decide: remain and believe the statements made by the commissars, that they would free Latvia or go home now. I said that I would drown myself if we did not immediately return to Latvia, where there was no famine or killings as there was here. The other children joined me, in a chorus, and the matter was settled right there on the spot because as father said, 'The future belongs to the children.'

---

5   Rīga fell to the Germans on September 3, 1917. In the Brest peace treaty half a year later the newly established Soviet government in Russia gave Germany; Finland, Estonia, Latvia, Lithuania, Poland as well as Ukraine.

The same commissars had passports made for us which stated that we were refugees from Latvia. This way, together with the real refugees, we could return to our beloved homeland. With all of our worldly possessions we were loaded into railway freight cars – and then – farewell Vitebsk! Farewell to nice and not so nice memories of living in a foreign land! Every part of me sang with joy!

Crossing the border, Paulis and Jānis became sick. The sick had to be left in a hospital, so we quickly hid them under blankets and piled the lighter bags on top of them. Both were babbling with delirium. The German border guard overheard them. What now? We began to chatter loudly and made busy with the travel bags, packing and unpacking them. The poor wretches almost suffocated under the load, but the guard was fooled because he thought it was us making the noise. When we pulled into Latvia just across the border everybody was put into barracks, dividing the intelligent ones (judging from appearance!) in one line and the others in another. Doctor Lūkins, who traveled with us in our wagon to Rīga with his two small sons, Ivars and Haralds, always poked fun at me. Suddenly he went up to the officer responsible for sorting out the two groups of people and told him in a loud voice that this girl, pointing his finger at me, must be put in the unintelligent lot. I began to wail and clutched father's hand – everybody laughed.

Did I grow up strong because I had to bear such wrongs? What would the psychologists who write about bringing up children say? When we were all quartered in the long barracks and in bed, I read the Russian ABC primer about the rooster with a golden comb. Doctor Lūkins walked up to me and asked, 'What are you reading?' I gave him the book. He leafed through it.

'This kind of book is not allowed for children!' he said, then he lay down on his bed and read it himself!

When my father, Doctor Lūkins and the surgeon, Alksnis, together with some other men began to play cards, a German soldier appeared and said that the gentlemen must retreat to the kitchen and peel potatoes. Doctor

Lūkins jumped to his feet, threw his cards on the table in a theatrical gesture, and frightened the poor soldier away. I liked that! Just like in the movies!

Then two German soldiers ordered all the men and woman to the *pirts* (Latvian sauna) to have a wash. In the women's section these same two soldiers stood outside overseeing the operation. I dug my heels in and refused to take off my shirt – I hated Germans. I pretended I didn't understand what they had said, but that helped little. The women tried to hide their nakedness with their long hair and hands. The water was awfully cold, so I just splashed myself. I didn't want to wash my thick hair in the cold water. One of the German soldiers grabbed my long braid and began to unravel it while he pointed to the water – lice were forbidden in Latvia! The women laughed and poked fun at the officers and I pretended I was washing. I quickly splashed water over me from head to toe and, shaking from the cold, I began to dry myself. Then the same officer came up to me and, smiling broadly, asked me how I was doing – I retorted, '*Schweinerei*[6].' That was the first and last bad word I ever uttered. I detested foul language and in future hid myself from the Germans.

Once we were back on the freight train we slept, squeezed together like sardines. Nearly everyone had diarrhea. The door of the wagon had to be pushed open and from the moving train the women covered the open door like a curtain and between them held the victim tightly until the victim had relieved herself. The men did likewise. The adults laughed all this off. The children organized competitions to see who could sit the longest on the suitcases piled high near the roof and not slide down. In this fashion we traveled through all of Latvia until we reached Tukums. But Tukums wasn't our final destination.

Father had gotten a job in Usma. While the train was standing at the station many crept under it and squatted to do their business. Me too.

---

6   This is a common German swear word derived from the word *swine*. Direct translation means swinish.

Then the train silently started gliding forward and I heard my mother's loud voice calling me. I jumped through the wheel and ran to catch the wagon's iron bar and remained there, dangling. The train was shunted onto another track and stopped. Strong arms pulled me up into the wagon, and just then the train picked up speed as it headed towards the Usma stopover where we had to get off.

Finally we arrived. Mother and Father, in a great hurry, first threw us out and then our belongings. The train couldn't wait long and huffed and puffed as it began to pick up speed again. Father jumped out and ran alongside the train to catch Mother as she jumped. To everybody's great delight they fell backwards into a ditch with their arms entwined. That looked so funny! There was much laughter and waving of hands to the remaining travelers in the train, which rushed away in a cloud of smoke. I jumped over the ditch, embraced the first pine tree, and cried, 'My beloved pine. My dear homeland's pine!'

It had taken us two whole months to travel the rather short distance from Vitebsk to Usma. In Usma, German soldiers waited for us with a cart drawn by two horses. We hopped into it and behind us a wagon pulled by another two horses, carried our belongings. We were on the way to father's new school like proud gentry! There our little apartment consisted of one sleeping room with one bed and a dining room together with a kitchen. It had a small table and two chairs that were so low when Vitauts sat down he upset the table and we all got soup in our laps. We spent one year in Usma.

The school was right beside the Usma Lake. Father taught the local kids the curriculum and how to sing and dance. Mother often sang while Father accompanied her on the church organ. Naturally, Vitauts, once more picked up his fishing hobby, but Mother forbade everyone from rowing over by boat to the fabulous and mysterious Morics Island in the middle of the lake.

Frost came in the beginning of winter without snow. The lake quickly froze over. The men walked upon the ice, which was like a mirror and beat upon the surface with axes. This way they stunned the big fish which were then pulled out. When spring began, the school went on an excursion across the ice to Morics Island. It was still cold like in winter, but here and there the snow had begun to melt. The birds sang and we could unbutton our coats and put our mittens in our pockets. The local guide showed us the foreign trees that had been planted on the island.

The ice was still holding. From the tops of the bank of the lake we rode our sleighs down onto the polished ice. We were not allowed to ride too far and hence had to break our ride. But, once again I had to try the forbidden. The ice caved in! I struggled with the sleigh and ice, up to my waist in water until I forced my way through the ice like an icebreaking ship and made it back to the shore. The kids stood around in great silence. I was freezing terribly, but I was also afraid to run home. Then one girl ran to my mother and told her everything. This time Mother was not angry. She quickly put me in a warm bath, then bundled me up in warm blankets and gave me hot chamomile tea to drink with strawberry jam.

Paulīne and her daughter Anna 11 years

From left: Paulis, Janis, Skaidrīte, Anna and Vitauts. Ventspils 1922

Chapter 2

The Long Distance Traveler[7]

Others returned home by different paths from much farther afield. When in 1915 the Rīga Polytechnical Institute was evacuated to Moscow at the onset of the war, Eduards Lejiņš, a 21 year old student from the commercial studies department, traveled along with the institute. Friends advised him not to be in a rush to finish his studies, otherwise he would be called up into the Russian army but Eduards didn't want to drag it out and he was awarded the institute's diploma in the summer of 1917. By then the tsar had abdicated and Russia was free. Military service was also compulsory in democratic Russia, headed by Alexander Kerenski. However, the young Mr. Lejiņš preempted his induction and volunteered to serve in the Provisional Government's army. He was assigned to an artillery unit and sent to serve in the former extravagant summer residence of the tsar's family in Tsarskoje Selo estate in Pushkin, a suburb of St. Petersburg.

When the Bolsheviks grabbed power in Russia through a coup d'état private Lejiņš was informed that he now served in the Red Army. Not in the famous Latvian Red Riflemen's Division, about which he knew nothing, but rather in an ordinary Russian unit. One fellow soldier asked him if he was related to Lenin because his surname sounded similar. Another stole the jacket of his fine uniform, which Eduards had had tailor-made when he joined Kerenski's army. It was worn only when he was on leave. During his studies in Moscow he had worked as an accountant at the Junker & Co. bank and later in Russia's Industrial Bank and therefore he could afford to buy better clothes.

---

7 This chapter is adapted from the written legacy of Eduards Lejiņš for this book with excerpts from the diary of Kārlis Lauks, who was a comrade-in-arms of Eduards in the Latvian national army unit, the Troicka battalion, that crossed Siberia with a Czech army contingent. Kārlis Lauks published his diary entitled, Troickas pulks: dienas grāmata par pulka gaitām (The Troicka Brigade: a diary of the brigade's travels), Toronto, Canada, 1978.

The Red Army sent him to St. Petersburg and put him on duty guarding the new Red Government and its leader, Vladimir Lenin in the Winter Palace. There, above the main entrance on the second floor, he stood with his rifle at his side and observed the movements in the square below.

Fifty years later, on his first trip to Rīga in 1970, his youngest son, Atis, already 28 years old, was traveling through Leningrad, as St. Petersburg was called in the Soviet Union. As he sat on a bench in the same square, licking an ice-cream, he observed the second floor, above the main entrance, and tried to imagine how his father had looked standing there with a rifle and Red Army badge pinned to his cap.

Nobody expected that the all-mighty Soviet Union would collapse like a house of cards just 21 years later in 1991. In order for his son, Atis to meditate on that bench about his father, the young soldier, Eduards Lejiņš had to survive the terrible Russian Civil War while serving in various armies, who were fighting each other. Then he had to make it safely, in an armed train, all the way to Vladivostok at the farthest end of Siberia.

Today it takes just one week by Trans-Siberian Rail. At the time of the Russian Civil War it took almost two years to travel that distance. And then together with other Latvian soldiers he traveled by ship from Japan with a stopover in Great Britain, where he stayed another two years before returning to his parent's home in Ventspils, Latvia.

Luck or Fate was on his side. In the summer of 1918 in St. Petersburg he ran into his Uncle Hamilkars who owned a student canteen. There, in turn, he met his cousin's husband, Benjamin Lindbergs who worked in the St. Petersburg Logistics Commissariat. Now it just happened that Mr. Lindbergs needed a good accountant and so, armed with the appropriate order from his army unit, Lejiņš was transferred to the Logistics Commissariat.

His duty was to visit the factories and check to see that animal skins were not being sold without the permission of the Lenin government. This was being done by the owner of a nationalized factory, since he could not account for the missing skins to inspector Lejiņš. When he visited the factory a second time, the sentry who stood guard at the door warned Lejiņš not to go home by the usual route after work, but suggested instead that he should climb out the window. The former owner had convinced the workers that Lejiņš had stopped the payment of their wages. He was told that he could have an accident on his way home and just happen to 'unintentionally' fall into a boiling cauldron. Lejiņš climbed out the window.

The situation in St. Petersburg had become dangerous and so with Benjamin Lindbergs, Lejiņš boarded a train and did not get off until it had arrived in a Latvian colony in the Ural Mountains. Lindberg's mother and brother lived there, where they owned a mill and a small farm. Here Lejiņš became a farmer, until ten months later when "The Supreme Ruler of Russia", Admiral Alexander Kolchak proclaimed mobilization of all men in the struggle against the Red Army, which, under the leadership of General Frunze was successfully pressing forward on all fronts against Kolchak and his anti-communist White Army. The new farmer did not heed the call to arms and was lucky to spot mounted soldiers fast approaching the farm. He jumped out the window and took off for the river where he hid in the bushes until Kolchak's men rode away.

However, one could not continue in this manner forever, so, in the end, he went to the town of Ufa to enlist in the White Army. He was assigned to the Alexander Gaisky division, but was spared from any fighting. The division, in horse-drawn wagons, simply retreated without stop before the onslaught of the Red Army over the Urals, deeper into Siberia.

In the Turgaya steppe, the war caught up with Lejiņš. Whilst having a meal the soldiers suddenly heard artillery shells exploding close by.

They fled, leaving all their provisions in the field. Lejiņš jumped on a camel, which he had been assigned by the commander to look after. This was lucky as in the bag strapped to the camel was the commander's belongings and his tobacco. Lejiņš pinched some tobacco every now and then because he had become a heavy smoker.

One day the commander of the division sent him to a Kirghiz village to trade sugar for flour. Lejiņš had at his disposal a horse and cart and one soldier. They duly went to the village, but at sunset, when they returned to their unit they discovered that everybody had vanished – wherever they turned their head nothing but the vast empty steppe gazed back! Both soldiers made for the nearest village, throwing the flour sacks on the ground - the poor horse couldn't cope with the load anymore. Luckily the commander had sent cavalry scouts to search for both "flour merchants" and they were soon reunited with their division. This was all for the better because if Lejiņš had been captured by the enemy he would have been shot by the Reds for being an 'intelligent white'. The settling of accounts was terrible for both sides. He didn't know what happened to the Russian soldier who accompanied him after they returned to their unit but Eduards Lejiņš was saved by the Troicka brigade, whose official name was, *The First Special Latvian Rifles Battalion.*

News that Latvian soldiers were being organized into their national units reached the ears of private Lejiņš. He went to ask for permission to leave the Russian White Army from the commanding officer of the Jayska Army Corps Headquarters, so that he could enlist in the Latvian unit. This officer turned out to be a Latvian, Colonel Kārlis Goppers. Lejiņš found him in the headquarters' tent lying on a couch. He rose to tell Lejiņš that he was no longer the commanding officer of the Corps Headquarters. He was leaving for the newly formed Latvian Imants brigade and was only waiting for news when he could join it in Vladivostok. But he kindly offered to write a letter of recommendation to the corps new commander, who received Lejiņš politely, and after hearing him out, discharged him from the army. He even provided a soldier with a horse and cart to take him to Krasnoyardsk, where the commander of the Troicka brigade, Major Dardzāns, enlisted him on 22nd November 1919 as a senior sergeant. For the next six months sergeant Lejiņš' home was the wagon of a freight train which had two rows of bunks, one on top of the other, and an iron stove in the middle of the wagon. However not all of the brigade made the 4,000 kilometers from Kranoyardsk to Vladivostok safely. And those who did manage, did so only by the skin of their teeth.

A White Army general, named Lebedev put forward the proposal that all Latvians on the side of the Whites should be shot as potential rebels. This plan was squashed by the Commander of the Allied Intervention Force in the Far East, the French general, Maurice Janin. The Allies had intervened on the side of the Whites against the Reds and henceforth the Troicka brigade had come under his direct command and protection. The much bigger force the Czech Corps also came under his command. The Troicka brigade was hooked onto the very tail of the Czech Corps that was traveling by trains to Vladivostok. As yet the Allies had still not come around to recognizing Latvian "separatism", i.e. independence, as the Allies were supporting the White armies against the Communists. Unlike Lenin, who was ready to recognize independence if the government was communist, the leaders of the Whites would not countenance any kind of independence for peoples living in Russia. The Allies accordingly demanded that the two Latvian brigades be disbanded in Siberia but General Janin thought otherwise and allowed both brigades to continue their journey as armed national units through Siberia.

The Reds continued their onward march, coming closer and closer to the White Army and the Czech Corps. The locomotives often froze in their tracks or else couldn't be commissioned. The trains often stayed in the same spot for days on end. The Red Army captured a force of 20,000 Polish soldiers which was traveling in the wake of the Latvians. The Polish army had been racked by dissension which split its ranks. At times when all seemed lost some groups in the Troicka brigade, together with their families who came from the local Latvian farming colonies, deserted to the Red Army. Armed battles also took place. One such battle took place by the Uka station in the very middle of winter in 1920. A fellow soldier of Eduards Lejiņš, Kārlis Lauks, who later fled in exile to Canada after the Second World War, described this battle in his diary, *'The Troicka Brigade'*. He wrote:

"Around seven in the morning we were awoken by machine gun and artillery fire. The men in our wagon shouted – 'Look how Kārlis' name day is going to be celebrated!' We dressed in a jiffy, grabbed our rifles and jumped out. The Reds had arrived from the main highway and had gone through a line of trees and were now blazing away at us. Our sentries, together with the Czechs and their armored train returned the fire. The brunt of the attack was thrust against one of our sentry posts with a machine gun and a three-man crew at the entrance of the village. There, in several waves, the attackers tried to force their way into the village in order to surround us. But they were beaten back. Then in the final assault the Red Cavalry was put into action. It was allowed to charge right up to the sentry lines and then all, men and horses, were hacked to pieces by the force of the machine gun bullets ... we later learned in Irkutsk that the Latvians serving on the Red side were incensed by the prowess of our machine gunners."

It was rumored that the Reds' commander was shot because of the unsuccessful attack on the Troicka brigade. Was he a Latvian? Were the cavalry Latvians? Did they know who they were attacking? The Troicka brigade was mainly made up of the Old Latvian Rifles, veterans of the great battles on the outskirts of Rīga in the First World War against the German army, the former comrades-in-arms of the Latvian soldiers now serving in the Red Army. Did the little Uka station witness a tragic bloodletting of a small nation?

The Troicka brigade suffered no casualties. However, the next day with the temperature hovering around minus 40, many were killed or wounded in the battle of Nizhniyudinska. Men fell, torn apart by bullets and froze to death in the snow if wounded. If a train with the provisions unit had not been the first to leave Nizhniyudinska then the whole brigade could have been wiped out. Senior sergeant Lejiņš served in the provisions unit.

The Czechs were enthusiastic about the bravery of the Latvian soldiers. They recalled an episode in one of their previous battles as written down by Kārlis Lauks in his diary: *"The enemy was defeated except for one lone machine gunner that continued obstinately to fire at us. We understood that this could not be an ordinary shooter. Verily, when the gun was finally silenced, the dead soldier was discovered to be a Latvian."*

Why did this unknown Latvian fight against the Czechs? Was he not able or did he not want to surrender to them? His bones are now lying in Kazan. He had disappeared without a trace from his father, mother, and perhaps also a wife and children.

The Czechs agreed to peace with the Soviet government and let the Red Army defeat General Semyonov, who now led the White Army in Siberia after Kolchak. While the Troicka men sat in the wagons and played cards, one Red Army train after the other drove past them to battle, and while the men continued to throw the cards down onto a makeshift table, they saw the trains returning, filled with the wounded. What did that lonely, brave Latvian machine gunner die for?

The Troicka soldiers almost got into a fight with Semyonov's troops. At one point Major Darzāns ordered all men to arms, including the clerks. Sergeant Lejiņš was given, in addition to his rifle, two hand grenades. Positioning themselves on the roofs of the wagon trains the soldiers took up battle positions while the train inched slowly passed the railway station, which was surrounded by the Whites. They hated Latvians because they had helped Lenin come to power. The attack however never came; they were afraid of the "Latishi" – the Latvian soldiers' fame overawed them. But if a single Latvian fell into their hands, they buried him alive in the cold earth.

Eduards Lejiņš, together with the remaining 1,000 Troicka men, some of whom had wives and children with them, finally reached Vladivostok where they boarded a ship named, *Voronezh* in midsummer 1920. Less than two months remained before Latvia and Soviet Russia would sign a peace treaty, but the sentiment of the local Russians was clearly felt.

'Only yesterday these Latvians were ours, but look at them now – they've become proper foreigners, haven't they!' they muttered.

Soviet power had still not reached the 'Ruler of the East', which is what Vladivostok means in English, but the Allies nevertheless handed over the former leader of the Whites, Admiral Kolchak to the communists. This hapless man, having lost everything in the civil war, sought refuge with the Czech Corps. "Higher interests", however, ruled that Admiral Kolchak, the erstwhile "Supreme Leader of Russia", should have his life ended before a quickly assembled Red Army execution squad.

The Troicka brigade continued its journey back to its homeland. It boarded a new ship in Japan, which bravely weathered a typhoon in the Indian Ocean, and only the occasional passenger, who died of sickness on board, had to be surrendered to the sea. In the autumn the ship, gaily blowing its horn, slowly steamed up the Thames estuary and docked at Chatham, near London.

The ship was met by the Latvian Consul General in London who, upon boarding the ship, enquired if there was anybody among the soldiers who could speak English. Sergeant Lejiņš was the only one who raised his hand. While the others had played cards, he had studiously studied English on the ship, and was promptly appointed Third secretary and translator at the consulate. The British Home Office accordingly issued a residency permit for him. Great Britain, France and the other Allied countries had still not officially recognized Latvia's independence, since another White, General Pyotr Wrangel, was still battling the Reds in the Crimea and the Allies continued to support him. It was only when the remnants of Wrangel's troops were crushed by the Latvian Red Riflemen, whose sworn enemy was the tsar, were the Allies ready to recognize Latvia as a legitimate state on 26th January 1921. The Soviet Russian government had already done so six months earlier. The USA was the only exception delaying her recognition for a year and a half, on 28th July 1922.

In the meantime Eduards Lejiņš had rented a room on Gordon Street, not far from the Latvian consulate, where breakfast was included in the price. He walked to work and lived, as he told Big Ben, "a quite life after all the turbulence of the Russian civil war". It took more than a year before he got tired of all the paper work and decided to continue his journey back home. He arrived in Ventspils for Christmas with several sterling British pounds in his pocket and a smart English suit.

The Lejiņš family did not originally come from Ventspils, but rather from the Vecate County, near Mazsalaca in Vidzeme. There Eduard's grandfather and his Estonian wife had a farmstead and 14 children, of whom eight were still alive when Latvia became free, and all of whom were well-situated. They were: Jānis, Eduard's father, a timber merchant, Morics - a doctor in Rīga, Antons and Richards - well-to-do farmers in northern Vidzeme, Hamilkars - head of Rīga City Hospital's Economy Department, Emma – who was married to a wealthy farmer, Eduards - a wine merchant in Lithuania, and finally, Paulis - a renowned scientist, head of the agricultural institute, Ramava, and Professor at the University of Latvia. During the short-lived Latvian Soviet government in 1919, Paulis taught at the University of Latvia and for a brief period was its pro-rector. For a short while, before Latvia was incorporated into the Soviet Union he was the Minister of Education in the "People's Government". During the German occupation he taught at the University of Latvia and, when the Russians returned, he became the president of the Latvian Academy of Sciences. He was awarded the Lenin Order though he never joined the Communist Party.

When Eduards was born in the winter of 1894, his father, Jānis was the manager of a Russian general's farm situated by the Ladoga Lake in the St. Petersburg province. Only towards the end of the century did

Jānis return with his family to Ventspils, Latvia, where he became a timber merchant. He rented a farm from the Russian government with a 99 year lease, which he called *Pommerland*. When Latvia gained its independence from Russia the Latvian government gave him ownership rights to the farm, and when Eduards returned home his father gave him the farm. Eduards Lejiņš thus became a farmer in his own country. He owned 6,060 hectares of arable land, 2,480 hectares of pastoral land and .755 hectares of fruit trees, including a vegetable garden. He remained in the Latvian army as a reservist.

The farm flourished. Its owner only had one problem – women. The maids came and went, since each wanted to become the mistress of *Pommerland*. Eduards Lejiņš did not fall in love with any of them so, in the end, he sold all his cattle and pigs and henceforth grew and sold only hay for the Ventspils market. That made his life simpler and he didn't need a woman to help him with the farm chores.

Still, a farmer needs a wife and, accordingly, one hot summer's day when the hay had been harvested Eduards Lejiņš journeyed to Vidzeme to look for a bride on the banks of the romantic Gauja River. Many songs had been written about this beautiful, meandering river and he took it into his head that there he would find his girl.

Fate decided otherwise. In a county office he asked a clerk for the addresses of the most exemplary farms in the area without telling, of course, that he was looking for a bride. The clerk, however, grew suspicious and not long after the would-be suitor was overtaken on the road by the local policeman in a horse drawn cart. Next to him sat the same "observant" clerk who pointed him out to the upholder of the law. The policeman must have been unduly influenced by the clerk because his manner was rather brusque when he demanded to know who the stranger was. Farmer Lejiņš answered in the same vein, demanding to know who the policeman thought he was. Eventually, after an exchange of views, both men agreed that a Latvian man was allowed to walk freely in his homeland.

But Eduards Lejiņš was still without a bride. He returned home and sold his farm and in 1929 moved to Rīga, where his parents had settled earlier in a one-story brick house on Slokas Street. In Rīga, he did a refresher course in mathematics and accountancy in order to become a high school teacher. He hadn't the faintest suspicion that back in Ventspils he was the cause of a young woman's hearty laughter, and that this woman was the daughter of Kristaps Irbe, with whom he on occasion drank beer with at the Latvian Society's house.

This he discovered only after two years when he returned to Ventspils with his teaching certificate in his pocket, which stated that he was entitled to teach commercial subjects at high school level. Ventspils was like a magnet to him, he had returned there from his world travels, and now Ventspils State Commercial and Trade School opened its doors and greeted him as one of its newest teachers.

Anna bracing for a swim in Kesteri

Eduards getting ready for a swim

Anna and Eduards in front of their school in Gulbene

Chapter 3

Joy and sorrow in a new state

Ventspils

My father became friends with the Lutheran church minister, Teodors Grīnbergs and together they established the Ventspils secondary school. The five Irbe children and twelve Kalniņš children (Uncle Ernest and my father's sister Anete's children) were found in almost all of the primary and secondary classes. I was already 14 years old when news came from Rīga that a free and independent Latvia had been proclaimed, but then war began all over again.[8] Ventspils changed hands from the Germans to the Red Latvian Riflemen. In the middle were the meager armed forces of the newly established Latvian state. Classes at school were often cancelled. The shops were empty. Still, none of us were really starving and we were respectably clothed. The Kalniņš children lived with us in a small house opposite the Jewish and Baptist churches. Their parents, Uncle Ernest and Aunty Anete sent my father bacon and potatoes from their farm for looking after their kids. For a 'piece of bacon' my father was able to buy a piano. There was no end to the laughter, hullabaloo, banging of doors, and misdeeds of Rūdis, one of the Kalniņš boys. He couldn't be stopped. Once he broke the synagogue's window, then disappeared from school. This rascal, however, later grew into a strapping young man, the best brother and cousin.

All the children loved and respected my father. He liked humor and therefore easily found out the "guilty" party. The oldest of the Kalniņš brothers was never at a loss to find ways to lead the younger ones astray so that afterwards, when they got into trouble, he could have a good laugh. My father had a powerful voice. If things got out of hand at school, all he, (nicknamed 'The Beard') had to do was shout, 'What's going on here!' and everyone immediately fell silent.

---

8   Latvia was proclaimed an independent state on November 18, 1918.

In the beginning we had no Latvian books. The teachers taught from their notes. It wasn't easy but we tried hard because we were all big patriots – we wanted to be wise Latvians. The Russian language was known only by those who had returned from Russia. They were able to find out things from old Russian text books.

I was said to be the best dressed girl in the school. Aunty Anete wove me coarse cloth from flax threads, which was in a natural sandy color. From that my mother sewed me a simple dress and embroidered it with folklore signs and symbols around the neck, waist and hem. From the same thread she sewed me "net" stockings, while the cobbler made shoes for me from tarpaulin with an elevated heel made from wood. The soles were made from closely entwined string and the finished product was painted white. When I played the piano in a concert, my mother made me a white dress from bandages and stiffened it with a mass of starch. I looked like a ballerina with a light blue, wide ribbon around my middle, which was tied in a bow at the back. Nobody could outdo my mother in making clothes, housekeeping or in the love she had for her children and her dedication to their upbringing. There was only one aspect that other mothers surpassed her and that was in teaching 'good manners' to her children.

Sometimes machine gun fire was heard around the school. On these occasions Vitauts usually made for the "little room". Everybody else ran outside like lightning. Once when we were halfway home we ran into a cafeteria, where seldom one could get cakes, and never coffee. It had big, wide windows facing the street and I, along with a group of pupils and our teacher, crawled underneath the tables with our backsides turned towards the windows – like ostriches. I got the giggles but the teacher stopped me with a severe scolding.

Oh, how terrible! A German soldier was lying dead on the steps in front of our house with blood, like a red ribbon, trickling onto the footpath, down the gutter and into the drain. A bullet had gone through our window and lodged itself precisely in the breast of the deer in the painting hanging on the wall.

The Reds won. Through the window from the school's big room you could see a wide open field of vegetable garden allotments for the town's inhabitants. A boy was standing by the window.

'Quickly, come to the window!' he shouted.

I ran up to look and exactly at that moment I saw somebody being shot and falling to the ground. I was shocked. I glanced angrily towards the boy but he took to his heels and fled the room.

We saw through the window of our home a group of captured German soldiers marching past. They were being led to the forest to be shot.

Next the Germans won. Some pupils – "socialists" – were incarcerated by the Germans in the cellar of an ancient castle built by the Teutonic Order in the Middle Ages. We girls brought sandwiches for them which we passed through the iron bars. Father pleaded with the Germans to spare them, vouching that they were not communists. Years later these same left-wing youth became proper bourgeois citizens like the rest of us.

Valdis, the eldest of the Kalniņš children, had secretly stolen down to the harbor to watch how the Germans shot the socialists and the communists by the warehouses. Later he told us the blood had flowed as it does in a cattle slaughter house. Father would have pulled down Valdis' pants and given him a proper thrashing but this time he only told him off. He was so relieved that Valdis had not been grabbed and shot. Of Ventspils 3,000 inhabitants – all the refugees had still not returned – the Germans shot 300.

Then one day all the town's inhabitants, except the children and the old people, were made to gather in the big church square. A German officer walked past the long lines and peered hard into each face until he stopped by one woman. He demanded that she give him back the gold ring she had stolen from him. This officer was one of the soldiers that had been led to the nearby forest to be shot by the Reds. The inhabitants lacked clothing and the women took the clothes from the dead soldiers. This woman in her rush and fright had not been able to pull the ring from the wounded officer, who had pretended to be dead. She took the ring, together with his finger. The officer somehow managed to make his way south to Liepāja, which Soviet Latvia's army had not been able to take. Then, with fresh German troops, he returned to take his revenge. The woman was shot.

Ernsts Karpovics, the head of Soviet power in Ventspils, jumped onto a train at the very last minute and managed to escape to Rīga. But from there he also had to flee together with the head of Soviet Latvia, Pēteris Stučka because Rīga was taken by the Germans and a Latvian brigade led by General Balodis. Soon enough these unlikely allies, the German anti-communist forces and the Latvian National Army, which had grown in strength, began fighting against each other. The Germans had only pretended they were anti-communist, in reality they wanted to make Latvia a German duchy.

At this time our school's rector, Teodors Grīnbergs resigned from his post. All the pupils then gathered in front of his house, which was like a little castle, lifted him into an armchair, carried him down the stairs to the road, and in the same manner our strongest boys carried him back to our school, marching and singing. He remained rector of the school until he became Latvia's first archbishop!

From the sea, British warships blazed away with their cannons. At long last our good western allies had understood that the German volunteer army in Latvia was not so much interested in toppling the Lenin government in Soviet Russia as they were in restoring their old German privileges in Latvia. Our new Prime Minister, Kārlis Ulmanis had summoned all the men in Latvia, both young and old, to fight for Latvia's freedom. Everybody in the school was elated. My mother cried. Vitauts was already 18 and had to go off to war. Father, though lame, because he had been injured in his previous soldiering days, and couldn't walk properly without a stick, was now marching together with his son. Both had backpacks and were headed for the harbor. I ran with them, crying.

The ship for Liepāja was already there waiting. Our little orchestra 'Piltenes prāģeri' (The Musicians from Piltene) started off with the upbeat folksong, *'Where are you off to, my little rooster'*. When they reached the highest note in the song, the trumpet blew in the wrong key, furthermore, much too loud, and everybody started laughing. The ship's captain began his speech... Suddenly a man ran up to him with a piece of paper in his hand - the captain read it - then - beaming with joy, announced that all the volunteers could go home - our army in the south of Latvia had won! The Germans had been driven into Lithuania!

High School in Ventspils

We lived on the top floor of another house while the Kalniņš children were quartered on the ground floor. I was still my mother's "right hand" as I had been since I was eleven. My little sister, Skaidrīte and my brothers had to obey me. With the exception of sewing and cooking, learning how to do all the other household chores came easily to me. Skaidrīte was good at handicraft but otherwise she was lazy. Her task was to dust the furniture, and when she wouldn't do it, I would lock her in a dark antechamber. She was afraid of the dark, and soon enough was ready to carry out her duties. I wasn't afraid of anybody, except ghosts.

I decided to stop learning German and to stop speaking Russian outside of school. I was already 16. When the workers marched by us in the street carrying red flags, all the school boys went for them with their fists. I had no idea who these "socialists" were.

My girlfriend, Irma lived next door in a two-story house. Across the street on the second floor of the pub, *Draudzība* (meaning *friendship*) lived my other girlfriend, Erna. Irma and I decided to read all of Dostoyevski's works. But how would we find the time for this? Then it came to us. As soon as everybody was asleep, I snuck over to Irma's. Skaidrīte was very attached to me, and I allowed her to sleep in my room sometimes, on Grandfather's big sheepskin coat on the floor. I got her to unlock the door when I returned home. However she worried too much, waiting for me, after all she was only six years old. I told her I was no longer going over to Irma's and persuaded her to stay and sleep with Mother. Then I quietly ran over to Irma's, leaving the door unlocked. While I read Dostoyevski aloud in Russian, Irma sewed pillow covers according to ancient Latvian designs. (This was a small exception to my decision to stop speaking Russian – I loved Dostoyevski and anyway in school I had to learn both Russian and German.) We both chewed on either dried peas that I had brought with me or on Irma's dried apples. By two in the morning I was back in my bed.

Sometimes it was freezing outside. In Irma's little room though, it was warm and cozy. One night we suddenly heard somebody climbing up the wooden stairs toward us. We darted out like lightning and bolted the glass door. Through the lace curtain, in the moonlight, we saw a dark silhouette stop in front of the glass door. It seemed that our hearts were ready to leap out of our mouths at any moment. We held our breath. The man was breathing heavily. Then he turned on his heels and descended the stairs and walked out of the building, banging the door shut behind him. We heard the sound of the snow crunching under his feet.

By now it was three in the morning but I was still too afraid to go home. Perhaps he was standing there, around the corner? Still, I had to get home. I had a peek – the road was clear – and I bolted for our door. That night I had left the door slightly ajar. I carefully open it and – Oh! Horror! What was that! A big, black, soft, shape brushed against my legs. I couldn't scream. It was a big, hairy dog! I pulled myself together and waved my head scarf at him.

'Tish! Tish! Off with you!' I hissed in hushed tones.

But he began to growl and flashed fire from his eyes. Then I changed tactics and begged him in a sweet voice to go back to his own home – and he shot out the door! I couldn't fall asleep after that. I thought – maybe he was the devil disguised as a dog.

The next time I went out I locked the door, but the dog was already waiting for me. So we set off together! At Irma's door I ever so gently prodded the dog away from me with my leg and darted behind the door. The next night there he was again. I became suspicious. Why didn't I see him during the day? It must be the devil accompanying me on my clandestine adventures. I ceased going to Irma's. The dog disappeared as suddenly as he had appeared.

The Ventspils high school looked like a castle. When the bell sounded, the doors to the class rooms burst open and all the kids, as one, tumbled out into the corridor. In the school yard the girls kept to themselves, the boys likewise formed their own crowd. Two scoundrels began pulling the blue ribbons from my blond, thick, long braids. I learned to swirl around, quick as lightning, and clobber them on their ears. Perhaps they tried to test my agility? Then I decided to let them do it unmolested – I didn't care less! The boys stopped. I won – maybe they weren't really that bad?

We spent the summer holidays at the Kalniņš' rented farmstead together with all their twelve children. Aunty Anete was merry by nature as was her brother, my father. There was dancing every evening. Uncle Ernests loved to dance the *Polka* with us. At harvest time we all helped to gather the hay. In the evenings, dusty and sticky with sweat, we walked through a little forest to wash in the river. The water was warm and a little mysterious by the light of the moon, hanging high in the sky. Joy throbbed through our bodies and souls!

Midsummer evening arrived. Together with the farm hands we sat at the long tables in the garden which were laden with everything the farm could offer; beer, big brown peas and beans, and a wooden ladle to scoop the *kupush* milk. That is a drink where cottage cheese is mixed with fermented milk. Laimonis, the dandy in a white shirt and tie, stood and scooped the *kupush* milk porridge to taste it, but was a little hesitant. 'Don't hold up the show. Let the others drink it,' I said, nudging his elbow a little. The *kupush* milk spilt onto his shirt and tie. Oh dear! The indignant look in his eyes! I took to my heels and ran into the house and yanked doors open and slammed them shut as I ran from one room to another. Laimonis yanked them open and left them open. Everybody looked in amazement at our mad race until I ran with my forehead into a door, which was just being opened by Laimonis' girlfriend, Līvija. 'What's going on!' she shouted at Laimonis.

Poor Laimonis apologized to her and then disappeared. When the games and dancing began in the garden, I overcame my fear and lost myself in the crowd. Laimonis could not be seen anywhere, nor Līvija. From that time on he always teased me - but I liked Valdis, his brother, and he liked me.

When we rode sleighs at Christmas time Valdis always harnessed the fastest horse, sat me in the sleigh, and put his arm around me. My fur coat was warm, but his strong arm was warmer still. But he could also be mischievous. For example, that one time in summer when we were swimming in the river's whirlpool and I grabbed the edge of the boat to rest a little while. He pushed me in jest, under the water. I choked with water in my mouth and thought I would die. All of a sudden I saw Valdis walking in the wake of my coffin bearers, crying. Ah ha, I thought. Now you are shedding big tears, you villain, but it's too late! I was pulled out of the water and revived. Valdis and his terrified brothers learned a good lesson. But such antics went on without end.

There was another dangerous lesson. Once, Valdis didn't want to go riding. I talked him into it and off we galloped on fast horses. Suddenly out of the bushes his brothers appeared, riding stallions that were neighing in a most frightful manner. All the horses took fright and panicked - they jumped over the ditch and tore across the big meadow like a tornado. One of the brothers fell off his horse and nearly broke his bones, but I was said to have flown through the air for a good while, like a witch with my spread hair blowing in the wind.

And Rūdis, another Kalniņš cousin, a gallant gentleman and ladies' man, once so infuriated me that I threw him down on the floor and beat him with my fists until I came to my senses when I saw his eyes popping out in fright. Much later, when we had all grown up, we agreed that all the Kalniņš boys had been in love with me without being aware of it.

Of the eight Kalniņš brothers four died tragic deaths: Žanis was killed while riding in the Home Guard's horse races, Rūdis and Maksis were deported to Siberia in 'The Year of Terror' during the Soviet occupation and were never seen or heard of again and Paulis was tortured to death by the Communists.

All sorts of things happened at school. We were three girlfriends with our three boys. I was average height with a fair complexion – a "rebellious spirit", in perpetual motion; Erna was tall, pale and beautiful; Silvija was very tall, with a heightened sense of justice and was prone to blushing quickly. All six of us stayed together, even when we went to study in Rīga. Kraulītis was my dancing partner. When we danced the tango, everybody retreated to the side. There was a fourth boy who was madly in love with me; lanky and thin, whose arms and legs protruded from his jacket's sleeves and trousers. But he was a good athlete, particularly in jumping and swimming. In the next-to-the-last class he jumped one class ahead so that, as he admitted to me, he could finish his studies early and marry me. Once the boys pulled him into our class room, stretched him on a table and began whacking him. I was the only girl left in the class. He was alone - against six! I grabbed the boys, mostly by their hair, and jerked them away. My poor 'lover' was so ashamed and red in the face that he fled from the class room. The next day a picture appeared on the wall in the school's glass notice board. 'The Long One' as my secret lover was called, was pictured doing a pole-volt with one hand extended to me, clutching a flower (with the roots dangling), drawn disproportionately long in length. I was drawn looking down at him from the upper story window – my braids were almost touching the ground! In school everybody knew everything – who was in love with who, and who couldn't stand each other anymore.

The Baltic Sea. Jūrmala, the seaside resort town, was our paradise. Clean sand, big sand dunes – and the pine forest right by the beach! I often swam to the second "bench" (shallow), where the water was only up to my neck and I could rest awhile, so that I could swim back to shore. However, our sea could be treacherous sometimes. One time the wind rose all of a sudden and the waves went over my head. I pawed my way back, crawling more on the bottom of the sea than swimming above the water. My brother, Vitauts was said to have run up and down the beach calling for help, although he was a good swimmer, he was too scared to come after me. But my 'hero lover', the 'Long One' had been following me and pulled me by my hair above the water.

He was also the first boy with whom I had a secret rendezvous at a set time and place. I was by then in the last class and he was already a student in Rīga. He complained that he had spent two days observing my apartment without success, hence it was better for us to always agree to a meeting beforehand. I felt sorry for him. But if only he did not have those awful green eyes! I took Skaidrīte with me, because I was nervous - I had to keep my word. He was a clever boy, who was a pleasure to talk to, despite his eyes.

How beautiful the big forest in Ventspils was. In the middle of a meadow the sun shed its light from the tops of the tall fir trees down onto us. This was my cathedral. Still, I did not fancy these secret meetings with just the two of us. I rather preferred that the three of us went to the ice skating rink or to a dance.

Once a football match was held in Ventspils between the sailors from a British ship and our boys. Despite our best efforts in rooting for our team, we lost. In the evening a dance took place where the ship's stoker became the center of attention – he was a Negro! A real live Negro! We had never seen one before. He, for his part, couldn't help wondering what it was he had done to become so popular.

No, we never had a dull moment! We stood on our feet for three evenings in a row in an overfilled hall to watch actors from Rīga and enthused over the plays of Shakespeare. Our school's "Apollo" club organized lectures on science and literature but never about politics. My experience in relation to politics was only that one time when a school mate asked me to accompany her to a social democratic meeting, where Bruno Kalniņš, no relation to us, was to speak. He was one of its more colorful leaders. I really wanted to hear him. Why I didn't attend , I just don't know.

I knew one communist. I wanted to see how fishermen enjoyed themselves at their summer dances by the Venta River. I went with them in their large fishing boat and the communist teased me about capitalism and the proletariat.
'If all female workers were as well educated and as nice as you are,' he said, 'then communism would spread much faster.'

At the dance I sat down among the older women. I was amazed! Their witticism and lively spirits took me by surprise – they had something to say about each and every one of the dancers. Furthermore, our opinions coincided to the penny. I concluded that old folks were not so old after all!

I didn't like it when I had to play the piano in concerts. On the stage I was no longer "me". Biruta and Erna played the slow pieces, I took the fast ones. They read the music from their notes, I played by heart. I never used the pedals, because my legs trembled too much. I saw nothing but the piano keys. Usually I played quite well. If I got it wrong, I rose quickly and disappeared behind the curtains, for which I received a standing ovation! I could be an actress if circumstances compelled me, but the stage frightened me. I was given the main role in a play where I was to make a declaration of love. As soon as I said two words – everybody started laughing! The teacher told me I had the talent of a comedian. In the end the main role was given to one of my cousins, Milda Kalniņa but I had to show her how to embrace her lover, and so on. I had seen all that in the movie pictures.

I took acting lessons during the summer holidays. Our teacher asked me to 'correctly' read the poem, *Heaven* by our famous poetess, Aspāzija. Reluctantly I stepped up to the podium. As soon as I began with 'Oh, how blue is the sky ...,' the room filled with laughter. Our teacher couldn't stop laughing, and Milda opined that she could never say it as funny as I did. So, I could only be 'me', I couldn't copy anybody else. Poetry could move me but only if I could read it when I was alone.

We often crossed the mouth of the Venta river by boat to the other shore, where the sea's coastline was steeper and where hardly anybody swam. There was only the singing of the wind through the pines and a deep stillness. The ferryman allowed me to row, which I liked very much. He taught me how to use the oars, when the waves got bigger in the sea. How glad I was that I learned that skill!

One day some eight of us, boys and girls, hopped into a boat and headed out to sea, rowing past the moles on both sides of the river. Out at sea we ran, of course, into the waves, but none of the boys knew how to row in big waves. Panic arose. Three of the girls didn't even know how to swim! I grabbed the oars and shouted at the others to steer the boat against the waves. I waited until the big waves subsided, then shouted that I was going to turn the boat around, and that the rower behind me should pull with all his strength. What luck that the boy holding the rudder knew how to steer!

Despite this near tragedy, the sea kept pulling us back to it. Once, one of the moles had been breached in places and during a storm the waves swept through the gaps. Though it was dangerous, we nevertheless ran across the boards used to patch up the holes. In winter, when the boards were frozen with ice we crossed them on all fours. The distance was not big, but dexterity was the order of the day. One pupil went to the very end of the mole in a storm and the waves knocked him into the churning sea. I don't think it was suicide.

At Christmas we followed the ancient Latvian tradition called, *Ķekatas* and disguised ourselves as different people or animals. The stork, the rooster and the wolf were most popular. Two people, one standing upright, the other bent with a blanket over them, made an excellent horse. We went out dancing and singing from house to house and had loads of fun rolling about in the snow drifts. One time Erna and I decided to surprise Biruta's parents. I pulled on Father's boots, stuffed a pillow in my coat to look like a fat stomach, reddened my nose somewhat, glued on black whiskers and donned a hat. Erna made herself into a lady of ill repute. We made our way along the narrow, dark cobbled streets to their house, where, on the ground floor, they had a food and beer store. We rang the bell, but Biruta's brother would not let us in. He would not unhook the chain. I said that all we wanted was to buy a bottle of beer. Erna could hardly contain herself anymore. I rang once more. Now the second brother and Biruta's mother opened the door slightly and I pushed my way forward with my big stomach. They took me for a drunkard! Finally Biruta appeared, saw me, and set off gales of laughter all round.

Spring came unannounced and exams were upon us. So-called 'tickets', each with a topic that would be in the exam, were distributed and Erna and I went off early in the morning over the river to the old grave yard. Reclining our backs against a forgotten tomb mound we began to cram for the exams. It was almost dark when we had just about finished off all the 'tickets'. All of a sudden an eerie silence fell upon us... Was somebody observing us? Had we disturbed somebody's peace? We fled for all we were worth!

The written examination took place in the big hall. All went well, but I encountered difficulties in the German and mathematics exams. In German I didn't understand the meaning of a piece when read out by Old Man Stūris, who was very strict. We sat separated at a distance from one another at our school desks, but I had very good hearing and Paula, who caught my SOS signals, ever so softly whispered the meaning to me in Latvian. I had to fill at least two pages. Passing by me, the director of the school, Teodors Grīnbergs bent down and corrected my mistake. Stūris was writing something further away. The director corrected my text once more. Stūris gave me a 'three' but the other teachers gave me a 'four', only one less than the top, 'five'. 'Four' was the grade that finally appeared on my diploma.

In the oral test I repeated the texts by heart, but swallowed the grammatical endings. Stūris gave me another 'three', the others a 'four', which became my final grade.

I got mixed-up in the mathematics exam. I forgot to use a formula to solve an unusual problem on the blackboard. Kraulītis whispered it to me, and I, with my excellent hearing, heard it. I filled two pages, and I was the third person to finish the assignment. As Kraulītis walked passed he whispered the answer. It was not the same as mine! I stared in amazement – what had I done wrong? My dear old mathematics teacher, Mr. Stiprais came up to me and silently put his finger on one "plus" sign. I looked again and then I looked a third time and saw it. Instead of a 'minus' I had used a 'plus'. I got a 'five'. No 'threes' Everything went fine in the oral examination, then I could enjoy myself.

It was graduation night. The teachers gave their farewell speeches. My father gave the most heartfelt speech. My dear father! How many times had I quarreled with him: me the 'suffragette', the free thinker! For instance, I told him I would not get married if I didn't love the man, but I would nevertheless have children, because I loved children. But they would have only one father, and I didn't care what people said. When the teachers finished, it was the pupils turn to give speeches. It was a very solemn evening. Some girls, myself included, cried. The boys looked awfully serious. After that there was singing, dancing, and games. But Old Man Stūris sent his son, Visvaldis home to bed before the dancing began. The rest of the students, on the other hand, took the opportunity to relax with the teachers, to dance and sing with them. We washed the dishes at six in the morning so that the school keeper (who berated us constantly) would remember us well. We also swept the hall. One more farewell song – and we were off!

The next day my cousin, Kažus threw a farewell party at his house in the Zaķu village. All the village women pressed their noses hard against the window panes to see what we were doing. We couldn't send them away – such was the village custom. While dancing with Vitauts and chewing on small chocolate pieces I suddenly choked. I rushed into the bedroom and started to fight for my breath. Aunty Anete took fright and screamed for my father. His leg had grown stiff from his war injury, but he came quick enough, and threw me with great force over his knee as he plopped down onto a chair at the same time, while pressing my head down as far as possible. Suddenly I could breathe again. That was the second time I'd had to fight for air.

I finished school at the age of 18 and wanted to become a doctor. But I couldn't. For one thing, I didn't want to cut corpses. Secondly, the studies would take too long. My father took me to Rīga to ask for advice from Professor Ludis Bērziņš, his class mate from the Cēsis teachers' seminary. He said I could be a primary school teacher, all I needed to do was pass two more examinations, in natural science and anatomy.

'No,' I said, 'not for me.'

'Then what is it you want to do?'

'To travel!'

'Well, in that case, go and study English and you will be able to see the whole world! Furthermore, there is a shortage of English language teachers. Go and apply at the English Language Institute.'

Little did I or Professor Bērziņš know what this very sound advice would later mean for me. After a few months, at the age of 19, I passed the entrance exams and became a student at the English Language Institute.

Merry Rīga

All the teachers at the institute were English except for the director, Mr. J. Šmits, who was Latvian and who had returned from emigration to Canada. He taught the origins of the world's languages. In the beginning it wasn't easy for me. For example, Mrs. Ellis read a story. We had to retell it in writing. But her pronunciation sounded strange to me. Dolly, my teacher in Ventspils, did not speak like that. I didn't understand a thing. I was ready to cry. Next to me sat the serious looking director of the Seamans School. My dark eyelashes hid my eyes and I read his writing. He took his left arm from the table so that I could see better. Then it came to me! But I used different words from his when I re-told the story, because my skill in the English language was quite good.

Professor Wilson taught us grammar and the history of the English people. He made me write essays about nature, horses and house construction – awfully dull! On the other hand, I liked a teacher named Roland, a bachelor, about 40, who let us write what we liked. He was a real English gentleman. He had a rather dark complexion with cornflower blue eyes and black hair. His face looked as if it was chiseled out of granite. After reading my '*The Art of Living and Love*' he wrote in red ink in my book that I had the talent of a writer – a whole page on why he thought so!

'Can't you see, he is in love with you!' Paula warned. 'I had to tell him everything about you.'
What agony! He looked straight at me, I had to avert my eyes.

I also attended the lectures of Professor Dauge at the University of Latvia on the topic of children's psychology and their upbringing. My father got me a job as a governess with one of my uncles, who had a seven year old daughter. My task was to prepare her for her first year in primary school. Her father had a red face with brown, shiny eyes, and he was always very polite towards me. The daughter was blonde, just like her mother. They had a two-story house. On the bottom floor was a tavern, where the mother toiled and cooked from early morning till late at night. The girl, on the other hand, was spoilt. She had suffered from polio and her legs were still in braces. I tried to teach her how to play the piano but she refused and banged her little fists on the keys, and I had to whack her a little on the fingers with a ruler. She ran to her mother to complain, but her mother just said, 'You better do as Miss Irbe says.' Luckily the girl was talented and soon became very attached to me.

The maid liked me. My high school girlfriend, Mirdza Stūris, who was also in Rīga, studying at the conservatorium, came to eat with me when her money started to run out. The maid clandestinely brought me a bigger portion of food to my room. In the evening, when everybody went to bed, we washed ourselves in the bathroom. I continued taking 'piano lessons' from Mirdza, each time giving her a little money for them.

One evening the two of us decided to get drunk, just to see how we would behave. I bought a bottle of 'Pomerance' and sour sweets. The drink didn't taste that good, still, we managed to finish off the bottle. Mirdza then started to play Chopin on the piano, but everything went completely wrong.

'Bravo!' I shouted as I clapped my hands.

Then I leaned over, giggling, and to my great surprise fell from my chair into a summersault. Then we really started laughing. Suddenly the door bell rang.

'Papa! (Old Man Stūris)', cried Mirdza.

The fright drove our intoxication away. Mirdza threw the bottle behind the sofa and I opened the door. It was Mirdza's godfather!

'What a nice smell you have here in the room,' he said.

On the table beckoning was the lone cork.

'Well,' he said, 'you could give me some too!'

Mirdza showed him the empty bottle. He laughed his heart out when we confessed that we had wanted to get drunk.

Vitauts joined the Tālavijas student fraternity. He became a lackey as ritual prescribed and had to run around and do the bidding of the elders until his apprenticeship was over and he was awarded the corporation's right to bear its colors. Naturally, his grades suffered accordingly. But then I was invited to my first student corporation's ball. My landlady made me a modern, sand-colored, wool dress without sleeves, with slight folds in the middle, coupled with a golden rope like belt. A lace kerchief around my neck topped it off. It was a very elegant dress that could be worn in all seasons. The landlord gave me ten lats. All that as a Christmas present. I was prepared to dance the night away with students from the upper cream of society.

I sat. Vitauts stood next to me. We both observed the couples dancing on the floor.

'Why must I dance only with you, brother of mine?' I asked him.

'It's because you belong to the invisible caste. Only those with colors dance with the daughters of rich mothers.'

Finally Vitauts introduced me to another lackey. A country product, as could be seen by his suit. We danced. He kept stepping on my beautiful, new, sand-colored, high-heeled shoes. He offered me grapes. I refused – I felt unhappy. His face reddened. I felt sorry for him. Then I accustomed my feet to his clumsy steps. I danced with him all through the evening, only him. He was pretty smart. Later this man became the Latvian consul in Finland.

I wanted to be free like Vitauts and therefore I begged my parents to give me subsistence money so I didn't have to keep working as a governess. They agreed and I lived with Vitauts in one room, in Āgenskalns and elsewhere in Pārdaugava (the other half of Rīga, across the Daugava River from the city's center). Once, when we lived in Torņkalns, I ran out of money for the tram ticket. I crossed the Daugava Bridge and had to go through unlit little streets in a factory area. Suddenly I heard footsteps behind me. I had ice skates in my hand. I quickened my step. The person following me did likewise. Then I had to cross a big field to reach the lights on the other side. I walked along the path which had snow drifts on both sides. I heard him breathing hard. I ran. So did he! Then without warning, I wheeled around with the aim of slamming him in the face with my skates. He laughed!

'May I help the young lady carry her skates?' he asked.

'No thanks!'

I told him to walk in front of me. He did that. He tried to find out where I lived. I didn't say. Then he turned into a narrow side street, lifted his hat, and bid me farewell.

'Good night, honorable young lady!'

'Good night.'

Erna was studying history in Rīga and Silvija was working in an office. We skated in the evenings in the Esplanāde Square to the music of a live horn band. The three of us still stuck together, and the boys were here in Rīga also. Silvija hit upon the idea that we should thank them in a 'special way' for their friendship, that is, each one of us should kiss one of them. It was decided by lottery that she must kiss Edžus. Silvija, as always, turned red as a beet. She didn't want anybody to see the kiss so we hid behind a fir tree. She glanced around in fright to see if there was anybody approaching. Edžus waited and smiled. Finally! We made merry about her shyness!

At the student dances Kraulītis and I danced our famous tango until the break of dawn. Silvija and Erna scolded me for letting him take me home in a taxi. I was ready to take the tram and pleaded with him to accompany me only to the Daugava river, where the ferry could take me to the other side (it went all night), and from there it wasn't far to my home. He would have none of it and always accompanied me home. On the way we talked a lot, discoursed like philosophers. The distance then appeared to be very short. Once I asked him if he was tired of taking me home.

'I never would have thought that a woman could be just a man's friend,' he replied. 'And you are a friend to me, Anna. With you it is always interesting, never boring because I can never guess what you will say or do next.'

Once our boys didn't show up at a dance. Erna and Silvija got to have a dance or two, but nobody asked me for a dance. I looked too young, like a high-school girl! Ah, the ladies' waltz! I had already spied a good dancer in coat tails and invited him to dance with me. He gave me an off-hand glance, then took pity on me, and off we went. It was nice dancing with him but he was constantly looking around and singing to himself. This was revolting! Anger rose in me. I pushed him aside, and walked off, leaving him standing alone in the middle of the floor. Ah ha! Now you are surprised.

We often celebrated our birthdays. We discussed high brow topics all through the night. It seemed that the boys competed with one another for our sakes. Why did they need to drink hard liquor? With us girls, one glass of wine was enough. Vitauts, doing his apprenticeship as a lackey in the fraternity, needed to empty one glass after the other until he developed a craving for a 'little glass'. In my opinion a gentleman should never get drunk in the presence of a lady.

The liquor ran out at one of the dances. Still, Vitauts needed more. All the shops were closed. He disappeared and soon enough reappeared with a bottle of vodka. I would have to drag him home again! I grabbed the bottle and smashed it on the floor – all of life's expensive elixir flowed away into nothingness.

'My little sister, I will never forgive you for this!' Vitauts vowed.

'And I will never lend you money anymore, which you often forget to give back to me!'

Was I too hard on him?

I studied hard. I wanted to finish as quickly as possible. I became even paler (I was usually pale in winter, and in summer I didn't get very suntanned, although this was the fashion). Our parents did not send us money for things like the opera, theater, or the movies – we simply had to eat less. When Erna's brother got a job at the opera as a cashier, we had it made. We even got to sit in the box. Once, after the performance, he took us to a restaurant where you could dance and which was frequented by artists, ballet dancers and writers. He was a good sport. He paid wages in advance if needed and even loaned money from the opera's treasury.

An audit descended unannounced, somebody had not repaid the money back in time, and Erna's good brother lost his job. Pity.

Jānis Rainis' opera, *Fire and Night* enthralled me. I liked *Toska* best – especially when Milda Brechmane-Štengele sang. I liked all ballet. The 'Dailes' theater was more 'people friendly' – livelier, and you could get a glass of beer or a cup of tea at the bar. I never missed the plays by Zīverts, the Latvian playwright rising star, or Shakespeare.

We sometimes ate lunch in the student's mess. There we could have soup and bread to our heart's content. One or two pieces of bread found their way into our pockets. When there was no money left we 'visited' my uncle, the church dean, Kārlis Ernests Irbe, nephew of bishop Kārlis Irbe, who lived in Sarkandaugava. Having filled our stomachs we usually put off our departure until he asked whether we had any money for the tram.

'No, we didn't.'

We got the money but not more than what the tickets cost.

In the end I got tired of Vitauts' student fraternity antics, cleaning his clothes and 'famine'. I told him to go and live with cousin Kažus, who was also studying in Rīga. I wanted to help Silvija, because her brother, who was enrolled in the Officer's War Academy, had lost a whole month of Silvija's wages in a card game. Vitauts was angry that I had given up the little room, but father also gave him a good talking to about missing lectures. Cousin Kažus took him under his care. Vitauts pulled himself together. He even joined the student hockey team.

Silvija had one house dress and one work dress – for both winter and summer. On her head she wore a beret. I paid for the room, as Kažus did for his. In other words, Silvija and Vitauts got their rooms for free. Just as I shared my 'piece of bread' with Silvija, so did Kažus with Vitauts. Silvija was taller than me. Nevertheless in the spring she was able to wear one of my dresses. When we set off for the beach in summer, she pulled a crumpled hat out of the drawer, straightened it, and clamped it on her head, almost over her eyes. That was supposed to be modern.

I got a note from an old boyfriend from high school – he wanted to take me to Ķīšezers Lake which was situated in a pine forest in the posh Rīga suburb of Mežpārks. I couldn't understand why he unsettled me. We got tired from all the walking. He wanted me to come to his place on the way home to read his diary. I read it. I became rather cross. I thought to myself, friend, if you have to please your future boss and his daughter, then keep right on doing it!

    'Anna, what do you think?' he asked.

    'Nothing.'

    'Will I see you again?'

    'Maybe. Don't see me home.'

Was I cruel?

In my last year at the institute, Professor Wilson asked me to give a speech on the benefits of alcohol; somebody else was to speak against it. Entering the room, I ran into Roland. He took my hand – I felt happy! But outwardly I showed nothing. Why? What was it that always stopped me from showing my feelings? I knew my speech off by heart and everything went smoothly, but as soon as I said, 'He was an old man, about 50 years of age,' Wilson jumped up, clapping his hands.

    'Thank you, Miss Irbe, however, I do protest. I am 50 years old but I am not an old man!'

Laughter filled the room. I had mixed up my words. I had wanted to say 'older man.' The professor was in the habit of boasting that in spite of his 50 years, he felt young. I was given a – 'very good' for the speech.

In our first model lesson in English, Paula and I were given the task of teaching ten-year old children. We decided to quiet our nerves by drinking a bottle of wine. We were surprised that it had no effect. It turned out that it was church wine. In the class room Paula was nervous for the first half hour, I the second half.

'What was the word *vuf* (in place of *wolf*) that you mentioned twice?' Professor Wilson wanted to know, in the evaluation later, to the great merriment of the class.

Wilson was in top form, he strode up and down and pronounced that Miss Irbe had to be a little gentler in her class. He got the impression that the children were frightened by such a stern teacher. The director of the Seamans School defended me vigorously.

'Miss Irbe will not be teaching small kids, but adults. Furthermore she herself is very young.'

The last event of the year was fast approaching – the ball. Nobody volunteered to recite English poetry. Wilson was at a loss. No! Nobody would ever get me to climb up on the stage again! The professor ran up and down the class and abruptly stopped in front of me. I raised my hand. Elated, he named the day and hour, once a week, that I would practice with him.

'Home – there is no other place like home.' I liked the contents of the poem but four whole weeks of practice! I thought I would not be able to stomach it. Two hours of the same thing. From twelve to two. I left the house at eleven. He corrected my pronunciation and 'tone' and ate a sandwich at the same time. When I had forgotten to have breakfast, usually rye bread with a glass of milk, I indeed felt very hungry. He never offered me anything – scrooge! I recited the poem in the tram and on the ferry, contemplating the river's deep waters. I even did it in my dreams! At the last lesson he was finally satisfied.

'The pronunciation is almost perfect, for a Latvian girl. Wonderful! Wonderful! Thank you. See you on Saturday night. Don't get sick!' he said and then shook my hand.

On the night of the ball Professor Wilson sat in the front row with the British, American and French consuls and other bigwigs. Our choir sang Latvian and British hymns, and a few other songs. My hands were cold. Before playing the piano in front of an audience I always warmed my hands in a woolen hand warmer. I climbed up on the stage but saw nobody. I felt my knees shaking and thought that my beautiful green dress was also probably shaking above my knees. I got to the centre of the stage but as I began to speak my breath got caught in my throat. The professor, who was hiding behind the curtains, whispered the start of the text to me - as if I didn't know it. I inhaled deeply and in an elated voice got through the whole piece. (Paula thought that the little pause gave the desired effect.) I became a star. Only then did I see the smiling faces in the crowd. Somebody was even shouting 'Bravo!' It must have been Roland with the other young teacher, his friend, because before the start bell rang, I got the impression they were just a little too happy – they had most probably 'strengthened' themselves with a glass or two.

The music started – the *Polonaise* – the professor himself led. He solemnly strode across the hall in his coat tails and white vest, bowed before me, and I extended my hand to him. He commanded in French. I felt elated. Afterwards I danced with the boys from my class, with the director of the Seamans School, and with the new English language teacher. Roland stood glumly by and watched with his back against the wall. Dancing past, I waved to him, and he smiled. Why not? Tonight I was happy! He had a red rose in his hand, which he gave to me later.

The final exams arrived. I studied until three in the morning with a wet towel tied around my head to keep me awake. The landlady fed me hot broth for three days. There were written exams on Macbeth, English history and grammar. We had already passed other, less important tests in our class room work. Everything went smoothly except in history with Wilson. I couldn't remember the year the *Magna Charta* was signed. There were only two of us left, Wilson and I. The professor walked restlessly about the class room and I became nervous.

'Miss Irbe, I am hungry. How long am I going to have to wait until you decide to finish your paper?' Then he told me – 1215.
My final grades: Knowledge 5, and Pronunciation, the same. I fell asleep in the tram on the way home and ended up at the final stop. The

conductor woke me. I asked him to take me back and wake me at Slokas Street.

There was a farewell evening at the English club. Speeches, biscuits and wine. What a wonderful evening! I was dressed in a beautiful see-through, two-layered, dress in a light pink color, sleeveless with light grey stripes along the hem. I had light grey, high-heeled shoes and a wide-brimmed straw hat. Roland was keeping Paula and I company. He'd had something to drink and was very witty. When it was time for him to go he didn't want to let go so easily. At five in the morning I walked the streets alone - I didn't want to wait for the tram. I had hardly left the Old Town with its silent cobbled little streets when a thunder storm erupted and I got drenched to the skin by the warm rain. I took off my shoes, hid my hat beneath my dress and petticoat, and ran towards the river. I had my diploma in my handbag and I was only 21 years old – free and strong and soon I would return to my beloved Baltic sea. My parents had a little house and garden by the Ventspils harbor, where, when there was a fog I could hear the lighthouse's warning signal as the ships announced their comings and goings.

Some time later I received a card from Roland. He ended his message with *'You will be a star of Latvia one day. You can write!'* Later still his friend wrote to me to tell me that Roland had become an alcoholic and had been put in a clinic, where he died. He had shot himself.

My teaching career

I wanted to take it easy for a while and began working in the Ventspils harbor's administration office. It was very boring. In the afternoon I taught English to adults. Forty registered, but only twenty finished the course – all of whom were men. After three months I quit my office job and began teaching English in the gymnasium[9], where it was a required subject. I began my teaching career at the age of twenty two. I wore a short dress and braids that were tied in one heavy knot at the back of my

---

9 This is the term for high-school used in Europe.

head, which was quite uncomfortable. The older pupils remembered me from earlier days when I had been a pupil and, seeing me, grinned. They watched every move I made.

One day the gymnasium boys were marching along the street, under the leadership of their military instructor. As soon as they saw me, the bigger boys whispered something and then one of them started to sing, *'Anna, fair Anna, hand me the sauna's dipper, so I can better flap myself with the birch switch.'* Oh, how I wanted to look older like the other teachers; Miss Kauss, Miss Salmiņa, Miss Kersele, Miss Jakobsone, and Miss Lūse, all of whom were spinsters. I mentioned this incident to the director, Teodors Grīnbergs, and I had never seen him so angry. The boys got frightened and apologized to me.

The head of harbor administration, Mr. Dinbergs, was a good friend of my father's. Both were popular personalities. They diligently attended all events at the Latvian Society house and just as diligently emptied their beer jugs. Walking together along the street, one limped to one side, the other to the other side – both had walking sticks. But when they returned home they took the horse-drawn cabby. Late one night I heard clip, clop, clip, clop… and then the horse stopped. Father was haggling with the driver over the fare. I listened in anger. I had to get up and let father in. He put his arm around me and almost bent me down to the floor until I got him to his bed. I helped him get under the covers and listened to him lament that mother didn't care for him anymore. After I scolded him for talking nonsense in the middle of the night he queried, 'Don't you love me anymore?'
'Of course I love you Daddy. Now go to sleep.'

My father retired and left his post as school inspector. He accepted a job as an organ player in the Mežotne church in Zemgale. Since he had a fairly decent pension and since the law prohibited a pensioner from receiving a wage together with a pension, the church donated a piece of land to him instead with a beautiful orchard. We called the little farm *Ķesteri*. Father rented out the property, but he and my mother looked after the orchard, growing beautiful flowers; dahlias, gillyflowers, and others, during the summer.

Once again I had become my mother's 'right hand' even though I was now a teacher and leader of the girl scouts. The four of us, Mother, Skaidrīte, Grandfather and I, lived alone in the winter in Ventspils in a little house with a garden on Vasarnīcu Street, close to the sea and the forest, while my father stayed in Mežotne. At night, when I was in bed, the sound of the sea lulled me into a deep sleep. Mother and Skaidrīte – who was now a pupil at the gymnasium – were quartered on the ground floor. Grandfather and I lived upstairs. When I opened the window in my room in the spring, the lilac blossoms reached out to welcome me – the garden was a sea of blossom. My head became dizzy from the many scents. Grandfather wouldn't let up until the red entrance doors down stairs had been painted white – he couldn't stand the 'socialist' color! When Skaidrīte finished school she got a job in the Agricultural Academy's laboratory in Mežotne's castle. Then my mother joined my father and took over the running of the house and garden in Mežotne.

The harbor workers went on strike. Students from the Rīga University fraternities arrived as strike breakers. The girls from the gymnasium received them as heroes. Students! It meant we had great dancing! Milda was now a teacher at a primary school, measured in her movements and sensible. At the dance we sat and observed the boys. A student from the countryside bowed and invited Milda to dance. He pulled her into such a fiery polka, around and around the dance floor, that her hair unraveled and fell onto her shoulders. Then he danced a fast waltz with me. I felt like I was being carried! Dance after dance. He had forgotten about Milda. I began to get tired, though he was a splendid dancer and was practically holding me in the air with his strong arms. I rested my arm firmly on his shoulder. What was that? My hand became wet. I looked up. His collar had turned into a white, wet, wrapper around his neck! One cannot go home in that condition on a cool night. We decided that he would have to stay overnight at Milda's, who had two rooms on Vasarnīcu Street. We took off his suit, and Milda wrapped him up in a warm woolen blanket and then threw a coat over him. But the next morning Milda took fright – what would the neighbors say? The young man was obliged to sneak out of her dwelling unseen.

Milda had a strange dream. She saw glowing red coals placed on the floor at her feet. I was supposed to have come and picked up one piece after the other, leaving her with none. But was it my fault he wanted to dance only with me?

After a year, when the Ventspils commercial school was established, I went to work there. English was a required subject from the first class, also in the trade school, which was in the same building, in the seamans section. There was plenty to do. I corrected assignments until one in the morning. The girl scout troop had also grown bigger. Two older girls assisted me in running the troop, but I had to devise the scout events and curricula. King George of Great Britain died and I had to give a speech about his life. I had very good diction and my voice could be heard in the farthest corner of the hall.

Kraulītis came home on holidays to visit his parents. Once again we danced the tango. I also danced with the pupils; maybe they entertained thoughts that if they danced with me all the time they would get higher grades? One cold winter's night I couldn't be bothered putting on my knitted woolen socks and sweater under my coat to go home after a dance. I caught a terrible cold and my lungs became inflamed. I lost weight, but finally pulled through and regained my weight by spending my summer holidays with my family in Mežotne.

Vitauts married Austra and it was a beautiful wedding. The church organ played the wedding march, and both of them, as if in slow motion, approached the altar. Vitauts' face was calm - Austra's pale from nerves. They walked between two rows of burning candles. The fraternity members formed a roof over their heads with their rapiers. On one side stood Austra's family and friends, on the other side the Irbe's. We cried.

I got a queer feeling that it was their march of sorrow. Why? Mudīte, their first daughter, would die at age four. And then they were deported to Siberia in 1941 when the Soviet Union occupied Latvia. We never saw them again.

At Christmas time I hopped on the train and was off to Rīga! With Vitauts and Austra we had one long ball. The opera, the theater, the movies, dances… I paid for Erna and Silvija, so they could join us. The newly wed couple lived in Austra's parent's house where Austra's sister, Elvīra lived with her husband. One of Austra's brothers lived in another room, where he was convalescing from tuberculosis. Austra's parents owned a number of buildings and were supposed to be 'capitalists'.

At one party Austra and Vitauts' then three year old daughter, Mudīte let out a little fart. Silence descended around the long table where the guests were seated. Poor Mudīte was unhappy. My grandfather stepped in.
  'Try once more. Try!' he said.
Mudīte did as she was told, filled her cheeks with air, and did her best. Nothing came of it. She then turned to Grandfather.
  'Try yourself!' she pouted to everybody's glee and amusement.

As always I played dance pieces on the piano. Everybody else danced. Kugrēns, a fraternity chap, a massive boy from the countryside with good natured blue eyes and dark hair, leant on the piano with his elbow and didn't take his eyes off me all evening. He didn't dance much, but in the *rotaļas* (dancing games) he didn't leave my side. How warmly and delicately he held my hand in his big paw as we went around in the dance circle!

In the summer, Vitauts, Austra and I were invited by Kugrēns' parents to their country house – it was as big as a manor! The lady of the house herself showed me all around the house and grounds.
  'Where are the horses?' I queried.
  'Out grazing in the paddocks.'

'What abundance!' I exclaimed.

'Wouldn't you like to become the mistress of this house?' she asked.

'Oh, no! I'm just a city mouse. I don't even know how to milk cows!'

'You wouldn't have to, there are milkmaids who do that.'

Then it finally dawned on me. She was waiting for my answer and lovingly kept her eyes on me. I felt terrible and couldn't say anything. She smiled and put her arm around my shoulder.

'Let's go and join the others,' she said.

They were also deported to Siberia when the Soviets came.

I had been working for quite some time when the former director of the English institute, Mr. Šmits invited me to go on an excursion to London. We took the train through Berlin to Belgium, but once we arrived in the capital of the British Empire we never stopped running. Wearily I often returned to the hotel with my shoes in my hand and just bare feet. The boys organized 'whiskey parties' in their rooms. My female companion took great care to see that I didn't fall into the boy's 'claws'. She and the others didn't hesitate for one minute in joining the parties, but as soon as she saw me coming through the door, she pushed me out with the admonishment to, 'Go to sleep, otherwise the boys will get you drunk, and after that anything could happen.'

But the reverse happened. The boys steered her out the door, and the other girls and I stayed. For the first time I was offered a glass of whisky. I took a sip and right away spat it back into the glass. One was supposed to mix it with water! But even then it wasn't to my liking. We sat and exchanged our impressions of London. We went to bed at twelve, because at six we had to be up again. The next day we had an invitation from the Lord Mayor of the city to visit London City Hall. A duchess was to address us there.

The orchestra was playing and we had to stand as we ate from a large stone table. There was not a chair in sight. My feet were hurting and I whispered to an English lad to fetch me a chair, because my new shoes were tormenting me. He asked me to follow him to search for one. We walked along a corridor with historical paintings hanging on the wall, and famous men and maybe also women laying silent in their sarcophagi. Finally we found a chair and I pulled off my shoes while he sat on the floor. What luck to be able to talk with a real English student! But then I woke up, perhaps the others had gone! I tried to put my shoes back on but they didn't fit anymore. I had bought them really too small. We both ran back.

'Bye, bye!'

I joined the others and we started off for the hotel, but we couldn't find the underground tube station. We were all hungry. We stopped by a movie theater, where a good-looking English boy looked at me carrying my shoes in my hand. I had a nice, light blue dress on and my golden locks reached my shoulders.

'Where could we eat that won't cost a fortune?' I asked.

There were the four of us girls. I studied his calloused hands, and it occurred to me that he must be a ship's stoker. He offered to take us to a place right across the street, because it was not appropriate for ladies to be unaccompanied by a gentleman. We ate delicious sandwiches and drank tea. He paid the bill, thanked us for our company, and showed us the way to the closest metro.

'Bye, bye…'

However, in the underground railway we got lost and traveled back and forth without end. Big Ben told us it was already two in the morning. We asked a woman how to get back to our hotel. She got in the train with us and put us on the right line. What amazing hospitality from a little, old, washer woman!

On the way back to Rīga we spent three hectic days in Berlin. In my group there was a daughter of a wealthy family and her brother and four students. We wanted to stay longer and Mr. Šmits gave us permission on the condition that I take responsibility for the group – me, who was by appearance the youngest! The consul fixed the necessary papers and so we stayed four more days. We went everywhere, the fun places, merry-go-rounds, the zoo… On the last night the boys told us we could go to bed, they still had to see something. The wealthy daughter would not accept that.

'Anna and I want to come along. Furthermore, you will not have to pay for us,' she said.

So off we all went to a seaman's pub. Everything was covered in red velvet. The boxes had curtains, some were drawn, and others were parted. As we danced, we peeked through a drawn curtain – inside a couple were kissing. We had sausages, sour cabbage, and beer – there was everything you could want. The room was filled with smoke. At one end there was a huge cupboard with a curtain. The curtain parted and a fat woman appeared wearing a big hat and ostrich feathers. Around her waist she had a black velvet band with a golden medal, black gloves up to her elbows and black stockings with garters and black high-heeled shoes. Apart from that she was completely naked. She had loads of make-up – perhaps she was about fifty. Horrid. We were not amused. We left, but the boys were angry. They had wanted to stay but they had to escort us back to the hotel. We returned in silence.

In the morning I had a headache and felt rotten. I headed to the local park and sat down on a bench, and without knowing it, fell asleep. I opened my eyes – where was I? An artist was drawing something and threw a glance in my direction every now and then. He was smiling. I got up and went over to him and had a look… There I was sleeping on the bench, in his painting, with my head pressed against my elbow and my hair hiding one of my cheeks, with my lips slightly parted. I glanced at my watch – the train was departing in one hour! I ran for all I was worth – there the others all were nervously standing on the street corner with my bags. They yanked me into the bus. We ran like mad to the sales office in the railway station, and then panting, hopped onto the train which was patiently waiting for us.

Every summer I spent my holidays with my parents in Mežotne. I had only recently returned from England when the daughter of Bishop Irbe, the second 'famous Anna', came to visit my father. She had married a Russian officer who had been shot dead by the communists during the Russian Civil War. Having returned to Rīga she lived with her father and young son, Cyril. Later she sent him to school in England and sailed for India where she became a missionary in the jungle in Koimbature, southern India, with lower caste Indians. She established a children's shelter called *Karunagarapuri* for Tamil children, which became known as the "Latvian village." Gradually she won over the hearts of the Indians by living a simple life together with them. She was supported in her work by the Swedish and Latvian Lutheran churches and died in 1973. A monument was erected in her honor in the missionary cemetery in Tirapatur.

Anna, the missionary, told us frightful stories of self-immolation. A fakir had seated several people in a cart which had an iron hook attached to the end of its shaft. He dug the hook into his body behind his backbone and pulled the cart without losing a drop of blood. Anna wanted me to return with her to India so that I could eventually become her replacement. I declined saying that I loved my country too much to leave it and was afraid to start something which I wasn't one hundred percent sure I could do. And I had only just begun to 'live a full life!' But would I, the third Anna, also become famous?

Before my trip to England my cousin, Kažus repeatedly tried to introduce me to one Mr. Eduards Lejiņš, nicknamed 'The Baron of Pomerlande'. But in the end he was afraid to introduce me to this 'English gentleman', because he thought I was certain to do something silly that wouldn't be to the liking of Mr. Lejiņš. Once Kažus accompanied Erna, Sylvija and I to the station. On the way we ran into a funeral procession.

'Look, Anna, there is Mr. Lejiņš walking in the procession!' Kažus whispered excitedly to me.

'Where? Where?'

'The man in the black-top boots, in the homespun green jacket, with amber reddish whiskers, and a hat on his head!'

'Him!' I cried.

I sat down on the edge of the road as if cut down by a scythe – and laughed!

'What English gentleman? Where is the English black coat-tails, stripped trousers and bowler on his head?'

Kažus got quite angry at me and wouldn't speak to me for a whole month.

Then one day the school's director, Mr. Turauskis entered the staff room and introduced us to the new teacher – Mr. Eduards Lejiņš. I was taken by surprise. He was dressed in an English pin-striped, brown suit – and looked quite solemn. Why did he hold my hand so long and look at me with his dark eyes? I moved my hand and he let it go. He revealed later that at that moment he thought, it's her or no one else! Once Old Man Stūris had said in a psychology lesson that an intelligent person, even if not well educated, knew at once if they were in love. Then a marriage would last forever.

Eduards Lejiņš, the only eligible bachelor, fell down like a meteor from heaven in the midst of the school's five spinsters. People said that he would marry another Anna Irbe, who wasn't at all related to me, and who had dark hair and cornflower blue eyes. She was beautiful and stately, as a mature woman should be. I, on the other hand, was still regarded as a student, because I lacked the 'teacher's imprint on my forehead'. One of my cousins hastened to congratulate me with a postcard on which was drawn a dragon and the inscription, *'Dear Anna, you are already 27, hurry up and marry – dragon Lejiņš is waiting for you!'*

One day Mr. Lejiņš, Miss Kauss and I took a short cut across the meadow to reach the forest, and what did Mr. Lejiņš do? He threw himself over a ditch, offering his back as a bridge and I, happily and ever so carefully and daintily walked across it. He didn't budge in the slightest! He has mighty strong muscles, as I have, I thought! But Miss Kauss assailed me for being inconsiderate.

Another time a boy handed me a list of all the names of the boys in the school who had fallen in love with me.

'Find out why,' I asked him.

The answer was not long in coming. The boys never knew how I would react to their behavior. I was simply unfathomable. But now another 'unfathomable' had emerged. I saw him all the time, but I pretended I didn't see him.

He gave a lecture for the pupils and teachers.
'He looks rather hansom this evening,' I whispered to Miss Kauss.
'He's shaved off his moustache, can't you see!' she replied.
Later on he told me that he had traveled throughout the land in search of a bride, and had found one. She was ready to come to him, but had said that he should first get rid of his whiskers – they were not in fashion then.
'Goodbye, my lady!' he immediately replied.

At the school dances I danced with the school boys and with Mr. Lejiņš. He had smooth, dry hands. He was elegant. He danced only with me, for he could not find a common step with any other.
'You have a different sense of rhythm,' I said.
'Perhaps, but you are able to adjust to it'.
He upped and bought everything on the buffet table for the benefit of the school! How he could pull off surprises! But he didn't understand women's humor. I once made a little joke about his work and quickly regretted it. How could anybody be so happy being a teacher! He was so enthusiastic about being entrusted with the younger generation! He wished to give them so much – and more and more!

He changed his suit every day, but I only had two dresses to change. One, an elegant light-blue knitted outfit and the other, a moss-green knitted dress with a sun-yellow stripe that ran diagonally across the breast. For summer I only had three or four dresses. I liked him best when he wore his black suit, but he didn't like my black dress. He was the only one who hurried to help me take off my coat. He confessed later that standing so close to me always made him feel dizzy. But I didn't use powder or makeup or even scented water – not even lipstick!

One day I discovered in my note book a note written by a pupil.

'You are my queen! Your hair is a golden crown. You are pale as if powdered white. Your eyelashes are black as if painted. Your lips are like two red rose petals.'

'Why, Miss Irbe, are your lips so red?' Mr. Lejiņš also once exclaimed while gazing at me.

Once when I arrived in Ventspils by train from Rīga, Eduards was waiting for me with his arms full of beautiful lilac blossom. Why so many? We walked without saying a word from the station, along the long road to my home in Vasarnīcu Street by the seaside. Then he broke the silence.

'Today I feel as if all of heaven is full of violets.'
I trembled.

That evening the pine trees by my window were sighing and the waves were quietly lapping the coastline as if with the palm of a hand. I put on a record and we danced. We stopped, our lips reached out and touched in the air – perhaps they didn't - my leg got caught against the corner of the sofa, and we both crashed into it. But I dared not laugh – perhaps he would feel hurt? What did he think? What did he feel?

The annual girl scouts big event arrived. We would perform a play we had written ourselves about girl scouts. Standing on the stage I explained to the audience about the work of our scouts, their excursions, charity work, and the world jamboree which took place in Jūrmala, Rīga in 1922 (and where the British general, Burt, tried to get fresh with me). I was wearing a short, green scout uniform, with my hair close cropped like a boy, one curl falling over my eye. Eduards and I danced afterwards.

'I liked you very much today – you were endearing!' he told me.
'Well, finally!'

There was a concert in Ventspils where a famous French violin player was performing. At first I was both elated and excited. Eduards and I walked up and down the corridor during the breaks. We quarreled and he became silent. I felt like I had been knocked off balance and felt unhappy. I saw a boy who bowed deeply and greeted me. My heart trembled. It was my 'lover' from my high school days. Oh, those green eyes! I walked up to him and took his hand.

'Please take me home!'

Our steps echoed in the silent streets.

'Have you finished your studies?' I asked him.

'Yes.'

'Well …?'

'I am a lawyer's assistant.'

'So …?'

'Anna, 'I'm not married…' he whispered.

We finished the walk in silence. As soon as we entered my room, he threw off his overcoat, helped me take off mine, and then I was lost like a little fish in the embrace of an octopus. I cried. Then it hit me that a terrible misunderstanding had taken place! I felt like I had given him poison – he was kissing me, but I knew he had to die. How could it be that I didn't realize he still loved me!

'I have waited six years for a sign from you, tonight I am the happiest man in the world!'

'No, I am not in love with you, and you've come too late. I love another.'

I made tea and we drank it in silence. For the first time I kissed him from my heart, because this time it was a final farewell for all time. He left quietly.

It was summer again. Eduards came to visit us at our little farm *Ķesteri* in Mežotne. He made his bed in the hay on the ground floor of the barn. Miss Kauss and I made ourselves comfortable upstairs on the top floor. Father bid us goodnight and grinning, told us not to be afraid of the rats. Miss Kauss and I both screamed! Eventually the conversation between the three of us petered out and Eduards began to speak in English with me. Miss Kauss got angry and went to sleep. Suddenly I screamed in fright! A 'rat' had landed on my nose. It was a big, velvety dahlia, which he had thrown up to me.

'Would you, Miss Irbe, allow me to have a telephone installed in your house so that we could talk in the evenings?'

'No! If you want to talk to me come and visit me!'
Silence.
'Would you like to become my wife and give us a little child?'
I was silent for a long time. This was completely unexpected!
Finally I replied.
'Yes!'

The next day Miss Kauss took leave of Eduards and I, and together we walked across the meadows, through a birch grove, to the Lielupe River to have a swim. Then we rode my horse, Ješka over to Bauska to look at the castle ruins. From the castle heights there was a fabulous view of the Lielupe river below. How beautiful my motherland was! On the way back the horse didn't hurry. We talked. Eduards asked questions, I answered. He was born in the previous century! What kind of world would he take me into? We were walking side by side and he was leading Ješka. Should I jump on my Ješka's back and gallop away, just clinging to his mane, barefoot, over the fields and ditches? Now I would have to do everything the 'right' way. Still, why did I feel so good and safe in his presence? Later I sensed his silent joy as I observed the movement of his hands as he pulled off my shoes. He had never been around girls because he had gone to a boy's school. At home he had played with his two little brothers and took them to task for making noise when their mother was taking her midday nap. When all three of them decided to see what doomsday would look like they turned the barometer's needle down as far as they could and then ran to the window to see how the world would collapse. It was Eduards who woke up that their mom and dad would also perish! In great fear they hoped they would not be too late as they shot back to the barometer and put the needle right.

My Ješka neighed softly. Eduards had gone to a former Baltic baron's manor and returned with an armful of yellow carnations which he laid in my lap. They were so beautiful! I hid my tears in them.

We put an announcement in the paper saying that Eduards Lejiņš and Anna Irbe were engaged. The flowers and congratulations for the most part were delivered to the other Anna Irbe! The inscription on the inside of my gold ring reads - *August 22, 1932. Teddy.*

On September 13, Teddy as I now called Eduards, called me from my class.

'Punktiņ[10],' he said excitedly, 'Archbishop Grīnbergs rang and said he was back from Rīga to make some arrangements and at two o'clock today he would be willing to marry us. Then he has to hurry back to Rīga.'
A pupil overheard this and got the whole school on its feet. He jumped on a bike and went to fetch beautiful roses from a far-away manor. Teddy ordered flowers and made sure that this time they would not be sent to the other, Miss Anna Irbe. I raced home and was surprised to see that long gladiolas had already been placed in a vase. How was that possible? Luckily my white dress had been washed and pressed, but one heel on my silver shoes was half-broken.

Hobbling, I hopped into the taxi where Teddy was waiting in a black suit and white shirt. The archbishop's house was like a small castle, you had to climb up several flights of stairs. Milda and Vilis, our bridesmaid and groomsman were already there. The archbishop, with the Bible in his hand, was waiting for us at the altar. We both had to step onto a carpet laid out for us. I remembered that my mother once told me, you must take the first step onto it, then you will be the ruler of the house. I glanced at Teddy. He looked so solemn, so deadly serious, that I forgot where I was. I can't remember what Teodors Grīnbergs, my director and former teacher said – maybe he said that the husband should be the head of the wife as Christ is the head of the church, as preached by Apostle Paul? We all kissed each other and happily descended the stairs. The whole school was waiting for us, and that boy handed me the roses!

10 Translated literally *Punktiņš* (nominative) means 'Dear little dot'. (*Punkts* means Dot. Latvians very often use the endearement form of a name ending in 'iņš', soft 'ņ' and the 'š' as in 'sh'.) Without the 'š' *Punktiņ* becomes vocative, but it means the same as in the nominative. English basically has lost the endearement form except in some words like 'Mummy'. Anna for her part used the English endearement *Teddy* for her husband instead of Ted.

The next day Teddy went off on an excursion with his class. We put off the wedding celebrations. When my mother arrived to make the arrangements, we invited all the teachers and our friends. They put their money together and presented us with a big crystal bowl with gold fittings, engraved with each of their initials. It was a wonderful wedding celebration – merry without any pretenses, quite childish with its goings on. We all jumped onto the big sofa in order to see how wide it was. Since the womenfolk hesitated, the men yanked the ladies after them. The uproarious laughter, screaming and shouting, was unbelievable. I would never have thought that teachers – the cream of society – could be such pranksters! Later my dear Aunty Anete Kalniņa organized a "real" wedding on her farm and after a year, on 18th November 1933, Ina, our first child was born.

The school got a new director and Teddy and I didn't like him. For the first time working at the school we both had trouble with the director and I started to get headaches. The doctor told me that the cold winds were the cause. He said we should move inland, far from the sea and we chose Gulbene. At the Gulbene commercial school we were able to teach the same subjects we had taught in Ventspils.

Gulbene was a small place, around 3,000 people, but it was growing. We got a two room apartment with a kitchen, at No. 28 Rīga Street. Later the owner knocked down a wall and we were able to live in a three room apartment with two kitchens. It was very quiet there even though the windows faced the street. My beloved white sea, so near to us on Vasarnīcu Street, no longer rocked me to sleep with the sound of its crashing waves. The pine trees didn't sough here even though the park was right around the corner. From the window I could see only trees with leaves and small fir trees.

The teachers and pupils were strangers to us, we had to start from the beginning. We were observed and talked about. The 'cream of society' invited us to a birthday celebration. The pupils studied well and were well-behaved. From the very start they applied themselves most diligently in Teddy's classes because they were afraid of him. The girls told me that the atmosphere was so intense that they begged me not to give them homework after they'd had a class with him. The boys still couldn't work me out – they continued to watch me closely. But I was now Mrs. Lejiņa and not the 23 year old 'girl' with a short skirt called 'Beautiful Anna' by the boys in the Ventspils gymnasium. I felt safe there. It was only in 1940 that we had a disagreement with some of the pupils. It seemed that we had contributed somewhat to uplifting the school and society there, though we seldom took part in the social life.

Our son, Aivars was born on February 12th, 1939. In October the Red Russians came to Latvia and set up their military bases. People reacted in different ways. Some said it would be alright, but we felt that there would be no end to what the Russians demanded and wanted. After less than a year the landlady rushed in.

'Russian tanks have rolled into Gulbene! It's the end[11]!' she screamed.

---

11   The fate of all three of the Baltic states; Estonia, Latvia, and Lithuania was sealed by the infamous Hitler-Stalin Pact, otherwise known as the Molotov-Ribbentrop Pact, on August 23, 1939. According to its provisions and subsequent protocols the Baltic states and Finland were designated as the Soviet Union's sphere of interest, while Poland was divided between Germany and the Soviet Union. Rumania's territory (Beserabia) was given to Moscow. This pact started the Second World War as Germany invaded Poland on September 1, 1939, and the Soviet Union did likewise from the East on September 17. After Poland was subjugated, Hitler's and Stalin's armies held an army parade together in Poland to celebrate their common victory. Great Britain declared war on Germany after the invasion of Poland.

During this time Stalin forced upon the three Baltic states 'mutual non-aggression' pacts which allowed the stationing of considerable Soviet troops in each Baltic state. Finland procrastinated in agreeing to the same demands and in the end chose to fight. The resulting war between Finland and the Soviet Union has gone down in history as the *Winter War*, and though Finland inflicted very heavy casualties on the Soviet army in the end she had to sue for peace. Stalin agreed because internaional public opinion supported Finland and Great Britain was preparing to send troops to help Finland. It is held that Finland's choice of war saved her from incorporation into the Soviet Union. In June 1940 Stalin sent his armies into the Baltic states while the world's attention was focused on the German capture of Paris and installed puppet governments, which, under the guise of 'democratic' elections proclaimed the Baltic states as Soviet

We were obliged to vote for a new government. Our ballots were numbered and we had to vote for everyone on the one and only election list. If we didn't something terrible would happen, just what, nobody could say.

Some of the braver souls, youths, crossed out the lists, but Teddy and I, along with everybody else we knew, voted as instructed for the new Kirchenšteins government. Not because we believed his promises that Latvia would now be a freer and better country, but because we were deeply afraid. We left the children at home with our maid and voted through gritted teeth for the abolishment of the Latvian state. Less then a month later, despite the election promises that Latvia would remain an independent state, Latvia was "admitted" into the Soviet Union – in just one minute an entire state disappeared. And both Teddy and I were completely unable to stop it.

Life went on. A circus arrived in town with animals. Ina liked watching the snakes and Aivars was just running about. Suddenly he stopped and looked at something. I observed my little son. His white head was bent down. He was standing in front of an elephant's leg. The elephant raised his foot a little and then put it back down on the ground. Finally Aivars began to move his eyes upwards. Higher and higher – his little head was now bent backwards as far as it could go, right against his backbone – whiz! He shot out of the circus and tore across the field towards home. There he was running for all he was worth in a white jacket and light blue shorts. I could hardly catch up with him. That big elephant, that was too much for him!

The children played as usual. Ina was the perfect child. She already knew the preparatory primary school's first year subjects and wanted very much to go to school, but when she got there the teacher didn't want her in the class. Ina was always drawing or writing something.

---

republics. This was quickly followed by their full incorporation into the Soviet Union. The reign of terror had begun.

When summoned to the blackboard she knew all the answers. That unsettled the teacher.

Ina had a 'boyfriend', who accompanied her home from school. Now and then I found messages in her pocket, *'Come to school. I have a frog.'* After half a year Ina became absent-minded. Once she went to school with only one shoe on. I noticed that after a heavy fall on the steps in Ventspils there was something wrong with her when she got excited.

One day she came home from school, frightened.

'Mom, the teacher said that Stalin is good and he is our Father, but our landlady said that he is a murderer!' she said.

I took her out of school.

Anna, Eduards and their first-born Ina in Ventspils

The Lejins family in Gulbene with baby
son Aivars and daughter Ina

Chapter 4.

The Year of Terror

People now avoided speaking loudly and looked upon each other with distrust. But we knew little about this because we had to work harder at school. One or two pupils were summoned to the new militia, which had replaced the police. I noticed that there was a girl in class who diligently wrote down everything I said as soon as I departed from my written text. When I asked her what she was scribbling, she reddened and the other students all grinned. After class a girl came up to me.

'Mrs. Lejiņš, don't you know that Zaiceva writes down everything you say?'

I remembered then that I had been in the habit of always giving one and the same example for "on": We go to church on Sundays. We go to school on weekdays, so that the "on" and "sun" (in contrast to "son") and "week" (in contrast to "weak") would sink in permanently to the student's minds. The local commissar for education summoned me because he wanted to know why I wasn't using this example anymore. I replied that now people were no longer, as a rule, going to church.

'Do you believe in God?' he asked.

'The God of the Old Testament does not make sense to me,' I answered.

He was suspicious about my connections to England because I'd once led a girl scouts group and had visited London as a student of the English Institute. Finally he relented and told me that my duty at school was to teach only English and Russian, to praise Stalin, and to teach that there was no God.

One of my former pupils from Ventspils, Miss Apse arrived to be my assistant English teacher. She got half of my hours, because I now had to teach Russian to the first and second grades, while my husband taught the third and fourth grades. I received her warmly. She later became the false accuser of an innocent Latvian – me – to the German secret police.

It turned out that one of our youngest teachers, Mr. Andersons, who often visited us at home and gave Ina chocolates, was a communist. That revelation shook everybody! The school council, where he decided everything, gave my husband the task of giving a lecture on "Dialectic Materialism". Would he dare say no to this "honor"? Teddy had been a member of the Farmer's Union!

A Russian army major and his wife, Pana were quartered in our apartment. Teddy borrowed the tenth volume of Lenin's collected works from him which included Lenin's ideas about this subject, the very foundation of communism, and began to work on his lecture. When did he sleep? After six months he was ready. His lecture was attended by the communist power elite and the teachers. Apparently it was good, because a few days later the county council asked him to read it again somewhere out in the countryside, but he had to cover the travel expenses himself.

This notwithstanding, my husband was summoned to an interrogation. There were mistakes in his lecture. Fortunately Teddy had noted all the instances where things appeared to contradict one another and had carefully noted on which page Lenin had said this or that. The interrogator was taken aback by this show of erudition. Teddy then had to explain that as a student he had read *Capital* by Karl Marx and that he got his Lenin books from the Russian major in our apartment. Next to the interrogator, a youngish party secretary, sat somebody else who tried to trip up my husband, but the secretary interrupted him and dismissed Teddy.

Still, there was continued interest about Teddy. Once, after school, an unknown person accompanied him home. He wanted to know why there were no communists among Latvian workers and whether the Russians had brought culture to Latvia.

Teddy was saved by the Russian major from whom he had borrowed the Lenin volume and to whom he had narrated the contents of his lecture before he had presented it. He had not only forgotten in his naïve Latvian way to mention Stalin's name but left out the very essence of it all, mainly, that Stalin was the greatest builder of communism. The major had pointed this out and the lecture was revised appropriately in time for the presentation.

I heard in school that one of the last grade's best pupils had accused teacher Lejiņš of being a hypocrite: He said Eduards Lejiņš was "a believing materialist". I was shocked. Teddy immediately wrote down what he would say in reply to this accusation when questioned by the school council. I was gratified by his answer, it was impersonal and factual. The council meeting began. The pupils were summoned and asked to repeat their accusation. Both parties felt awkward. My husband asked them – "Why?" They replied that teacher Lejiņš had put his hands together at the dining table as if in prayer and mentioned God. An exchange of words followed but nothing of any importance. The pupils were dismissed. But then Mr. Andersons took up the cudgel. He sat behind me, as always close to me. An argument flared up. Teddy suddenly jumped to his feet and approached Mr. Andersons. I felt that something awful was about to happen. I stepped between them and indignantly spoke about the hatred, distrust and foul suspicion that had replaced the harmony in which we had lived before. A deep silence followed. The director called out the next item on the agenda. And all this because of that lecture on dialectics! The pupils were national patriots and had wanted to set a trap for my husband. After graduating, one of them wrote him a letter of thanks. He had got a good job immediately and was praised for his excellent knowledge of accountancy. The other wrote stating that my husband was a hero.

Strange, though. Why did Mr. Andersons warn me that my husband's brother Jānis, a student, faced danger because of his patriotic beliefs, and that he couldn't do anything to save him?

Women were losing their husbands. Men were disappearing without explanation. My cousin Paulis failed to come home one evening. Later his mutilated body was found together with many others. Teddy often came home very late. I was sleeping very badly. Both of us had to be back at school early in the morning. The officer in charge of military training told me openly to expect terror. I warned him not to speak too loudly, as the room we were in had several doors.

'Just get into an aeroplane and flee!' he whispered in an urgent tone. The Latvian army was being concentrated in Gulbene.

The Russian officer and his wife, Pana lived in the dining room and the second kitchen of our apartment. Pana timidly knocked and asked if she could have galoshes to wear when she washed the building's staircase. We invited both of them to join us for tea and cakes. The officer carefully appraised our furniture, ran his hands over it. He commented that such sturdy, handmade furniture couldn't be found in his country, and when one did buy furniture, for example, a table, it was delivered with a broken leg or a leg that fell off right away once the table was put together... He stopped in fright in mid-sentence. He began to quickly explain himself, that all the furniture made in his country was not bad quality. He went to the radio and turned it on.

'Can you pick up London?' he asked.
But at the table he didn't take a bite at all. I had finished off two cakes before the Russians started to eat. Finally they began to joke around and polished off several cups of tea – and then suddenly the plate was empty! They asked me to play the Danube waltz over and over again on the piano. They had no intention of leaving. Pana begged me to go with her to help her buy shoes. When she went by herself the Latvian shopkeepers threw the shoes at her and made her wait until they fetched another pair.

'Alright,' I said, agreeing to go along with her.
The sales woman scowled at me, clearly the shop had been cleaned out. The worthless ruble had been put on parity with the strong Latvian currency, the Lat. Straight away our Russian pair bought; two bicycles,

two radios and a big box to put in all the things they'd bought. Pana was sending loads to her mother in Russia. She told me all of this. She also wanted very much to read a book in the Russian language. I found one on my shelf, an old love story about Russian aristocrats and gave it to her. She loved it!

I took a trip to Rīga. Pana accompanied me. She begged me to take her to my tailor, who made my business suits. She wanted something similar but more old fashioned, otherwise she would not dare to wear such modern clothing in Russia when she returned. In the train she told me how bad it was in Russia. To be sure there were doctors, but it took days to get them to come and by then the person had already died. She suddenly took fright – what had she said! She implored me not to tell anyone what she'd just told me!

My landlady didn't greet me anymore. I continued to greet her as usual. But the Russian couple also began to shy away from us. Teddy asked them why.

'It was now forbidden,' was the reply he got.

It had been pointed out to the Russian major that bringing a present from Leningrad in the form of a watermelon for the Lejiņš family was not appropriate.

'Would you like to work in Kazakhstan?' the major then asked Teddy. Without waiting for a reply he wheeled around and left Teddy standing speechless. Was he warning us of things to come? The major soon left us for a vacation.

For several days I heard nothing from the room where Pana was living. I knocked – no reply. I opened the door and saw Pana lying in bed, pale as a corpse!

'Pana!' I cried.

She opened her eyes and gestured for me to go away. I boiled some porridge and fed her. She hadn't eaten for two days. She was bleeding. There was a blood clot in her night pot. I wanted to get a doctor, but she wouldn't let me, saying that it was forbidden.[12] I ignored her and ran to the doctor on the other side of the street.

'Are you crazy? Do you know what you are asking? If she dies, you and I will be hanged!' he screamed. 'We will be accused of murdering her!'

'But you are a doctor!'

I didn't relent.

In the end he gave in and hurried back with me to Pana. He examined her and rushed back to me in my room, waving a prescription in his hand. Frightened, he urged me to get the medicine immediately so that all three of us could remain alive. I raced to the pharmacy but there was a long line in front of me.

'The Russian's wife is dying,' I whispered to Mr. Anderson's girlfriend. The medicine was immediately brought forward.

I fed Pana for several days and made her drink the medicine. Her eyes! How they shone with gratitude! But why did she tell me that she couldn't help me and begged for my forgiveness?

One morning I went to the window facing the road and opened the curtains. Officers in handsome Latvian army uniforms marched by as if on parade. But I saw that they didn't have their swords at their sides. How could that be? Russian soldiers with rifles marched beside them. I rushed into my landlady's apartment asking if she knew what was going on.

'Don't you know?'

'No, I don't.'

'They are being led to the woods to be shot!'

Fear and despair overtook me.

---

12 Soviet propaganda upheld the myth that the Soviet Union brought culture, science, health - in other words - all good things to the 'poor, suffering, oppressed and backward Latvian people'. Hence a Soviet citizen could not admit that they were in a worse state of health than a person recently 'liberated' by the Soviet Union, and, consequently, in need of medical aid from Latvians, who in fact had better health care than the Soviet Union had to offer. Perhaps there was also a double edge to this – Pana may also have been warning Anna that if she died, Anna would be held accountable if she had tried to help her and failed.

Because of the stress I could hardly go to school anymore. In the teacher's staff room I sat with Miss Apse and read. She opened a newspaper that had a portrait of Lenin covering the whole page. I looked at it and sighed.

'Nice eyes... I will be given a vacation and go to the Crimea and eat juicy pears because I am ill with consumption.'

Never would I have thought that these words, uttered in despair, would some time later almost bring about my demise!

Shame on you, Miss Apse, my lady compatriot! Wasn't the disaster brought onto the Latvian people by the Russians enough! And then you approached the German secret police and denounced my husband and I. You thought you were a patriot – what a mockery!

Pana and her husband had been packing all day. She needed some more things and begged me to give her a clothes iron and a cup. She appeared to be extremely upset. Her husband was being sent somewhere and an orderly was bending over backwards loading all their new belongings acquired in Gulbene into a truck. Finally everything was ready. Pana remained the last to leave. Hesitantly she opened our kitchen door, ran up to me, embraced and kissed me. Then she looked forlornly at me, began to cry, and ran off.

'What's happening?' I called out.

Pana didn't reply.

It was June 14th, 1941, the graduation evening for the senior students. I was wearing my best dress. I looked down at the street. Heavy trucks, one after the other, rumbled by. I was surprised to see an old man in the back of a truck suddenly look up at the upper window and see me. Our eyes met. I shuddered – that look, the anguish in those eyes! Where was he being taken? To be shot like the others? I ran to my landlady.

'What's happening?' I shouted.

I received the same cold response as before.

'Don't you know?'

'But why old people and children?'

I dashed back to my room, threw off my beautiful dress and put on my Latvian folk costume.

'Do you realize what you are doing!' Teddy shouted.

'I couldn't care less!'

Our housemaid, Alvīne arrived breathless, lamenting and weeping.

'Oh God, merciful God, those faces! They were loaded into cattle wagons at the railway station and were stretching out their hands through the bars with cups, begging for water.'

On the way she saw that the trucks from the dairy were taking all their milk to the deportees in the railway wagons. I put all the cans of food I had bought for the week in a basket for Alvīne to take to the railway station to distribute to the deportees. She understood I couldn't do it. I had two children and I was still a teacher.

'Never! Never will I forget what I saw. Blessed are those who were spared that sight!' Alvīne cried when she returned home again.

At school we found out that one of the graduates had run to school in the early morning and requested that his diploma be given to him immediately so that he could join his parents in the railway wagons.

At the graduation evening we were told to sing the *Communist International,* the anthem of the "world proletariat". I remained silent. I was amazed, the room was full of people but the song could hardly be heard! Teddy was only moving his lips without making a sound. The political commissar extended his gaze over everyone in the room and so I also began to move my lips. I was the only one dressed in a national folk costume. The female students looked at me with fear in their eyes. In a business like manner our director made his farewell speech to the graduates. Why didn't Zaiceva say anything? And why didn't Mr. Andersons say anything? Why were the communist youth not saying a word[13]?

---

13 Considering the large scale deportation taking place these Latvian communists could hardly stand up and make a promise to the teachers and students with whom they had worked with for many years that the Latvian people had a bright future.

After the official part of the evening was over we sat and drank tea. The students began to sing folk songs. The political commissar sat opposite me. He was merry, looked fondly at the girls, and made jokes. The students started to sing a very sad folk song about orphans. The commissar immediately demanded to know why they were singing one of our saddest songs. They were told to sing merry songs. The students obliged but made them sound like the solemn hymns sung in church.

'Why are you not singing?' the commissar whispered to the girl sitting next to him.

'I don't know the song,' she replied and started crying.

He whispered something else in her ear and then both of them got up and left. The rest of us fell silent and left the table. We never saw the girl again. The orchestra was playing and the students started to dance. Gradually, one by one, the hall emptied and the orchestra too, fell silent.

From our school in Gulbene, Jānis Liepa from the 3rd grade, and Valentīns Ore from the 4th grade were deported. From our old Ventspils school, Imants Audze, Alīse Stenkeviča and Miervaldis Zīlnieks were deported.[14]

I wrote to my parents to tell them we wanted to visit them on their new farm, *Viesturi*. They had sold their farm in Mežotne and now lived not far from Jelgava. I wrote the same to my brothers, Vitauts and Paulis, who lived in Rīga. On that awful black day of June 14th, 1941 the telephones were not working and the postal services had also been stopped. But I managed to take out, just in time, our small savings deposit of 200 rubles, that was once 200 lats, which were now forbidden. The new Soviet power in Latvia had implemented a number of restrictions regarding the purchase of consumer goods, but instead of buying a dress which was allowed, I bought a large piece of sturdy cloth and encased all our blankets and pillows in it. Still today I have a piece of the cloth that I later used to make a pillow and a piece of soap in rainbow colors

---

14   In the first year of Soviet occupation 30,000 people were deported to Siberia or killed. Of these, 15,000 were deported on one night alone, on June 14,1941. Similar deportations took place at the same time in Estonia and Lithuania.

that I saved from that day as keepsakes. We were making preparations to leave Gulbene because I remembered an awful dream I'd had in winter.

In it I saw my parent's farm, *Viesturi*. My daughter, Ina and Paulis' son, Imants were running around in front of the house. The bushes were just budding like it was spring. The windows at the end of the house, dubbed the "servants' end", were opened wide and the room was empty. The Russian couple who had been quartered there had left. I peered into the room and saw ballet dancers - girl students - in toadstool costumes, dancing. Shocked, I woke up with a start.

On June 14th, I told Teddy that we must leave for *Viesturi* by the next Sunday at the latest.
    'But we can't go. I have to coach those students who failed my class. Our wages have not been paid and our Russian passports have not been issued... And alone with the children, you cannot do it!' Teddy insisted.

    'I certainly can!'

I went to the militia, which had replaced our police, and talked to a clerk who was Latvian. He stated that it was not permitted to issue the new Soviet passports yet, and that in time they would be delivered to us at our homes. I had an answer ready.
    'But I have to visit my parents urgently, my mother...'
The clerk smiled at me and surreptitiously gave me the passport.
    'For my husband also,' I whispered.
    'Be my guest!'
Clutching the passports I hurried off to our school.

Comrade Andersons refused to pay our wages in advance.
    'No. I can't. Sorry.'
I turned into an actress and began to speak in a pleasant, sweet voice.
    'Just imagine; there I am with one child nestled in one arm, with a heavy bag to boot. In the other, a heavy suitcase and your little friend, Ina also lugging a suitcase.'

'Well, I see I can't get rid of you.'

He paid out. I was overwhelmed with joy and shook his hand firmly in gratitude. Later I heard that he was shot by the Germans, next to the Gulbene cemetery. It was said that he had refused to flee with the Russians.

A few days later, very early in the morning, I packed and ordered a carriage. I would need to carry a heavy load in both hands. Ina had her teddy bear in one hand and a small bag in the other with things she would need on the trip. Teddy watched us in silence. Then all of a sudden he grabbed the biggest suitcase and stuffed it with his clothes. He wrapped our bedding up in a huge bundle. We gave Alvīne the keys, money for expenses and the rent. The Lejiņš family bid farewell to Gulbene.

The train was full of Russian families. We found a place with the Latvians. A great silence reigned – everybody was wondering where the Russians were going. We got out in Rīga and saw more Russians sitting on the train platform, whole families with mountains of belongings all around them. They were waiting for something. We had to go and buy tickets to Jelgava, but suddenly the air raid warning siren started wailing! The militiaman ran up and down the platform shouting that it was only a fire alarm exercise and that everybody must stay in their places. I wanted a cup of tea and the children wanted milk. We climbed down from the platform and walked to the station café and saw Paulis running towards us.

'Anna! Anna! Vitauts has been deported with his family!' he shouted. We hugged each other tight and cried.

Vitauts died a year later, working in a slave labor camp in Siberia at the age of 41. His wife, Austra and their two daughters survived. After Nikita Khrushchev, the new Soviet leader, denounced Stalin and his crimes he amnestied all the deportees in the 1950's. Austra was thus able to return to Soviet-occupied Latvia in 1958, followed by her daughter Dzintra in 1961 together with her Russian husband, Valentīns and son, Dmitrijs.

Her second son, Juris was born in Latvia. Together with my cousin, Anna (one of the Kalniņš children who had married a Finnish diplomat) in Finland, we sent packages of warm clothing and medicine to Austra. But sending medicine was soon prohibited by the Soviet state. Her other daughter, Inta and her husband are now both deceased.

Jānis escaped deportation by the skin of his teeth. He was on the ship *Kandava* which had just returned from Leningrad to Liepāja with a cargo of agricultural fertilizer only a few days before June 14. He was the main helmsman and noticed that the dockworkers had been ordered to stop unloading the cargo and instead made to nail barbed wire in front of the windows and doors of the cattle train wagons.

He remembered that earlier an Estonian Jew who had sat next to him in a pub had warned him to be careful in the middle of June.

'Is war going to break out?' Jānis had asked.

'No, it will be worse than that,' the Jew replied.

Hence on June 13th, early in the morning, Jānis called the third mate and gave him the keys to the ship's safe and his packed seaman's bag which he asked the mate to send to him later in Rīga. Without a cap on his head or a bag in his hand, Jānis stepped down the ship's ladder without a trace of anxiety. Whistling a merry tune he stepped into the closest pub in the harbor, whose Jewish owner he knew well. There was nobody else in the bar.

'Down that and then keep moving. Danger is lurking!' the Jew warned as he handed Jānis a glass of vodka.

Jānis did as advised. At the railway station he bought a ticket to Rīga and then hid as best he could on the outskirts of town until it was dark. Minutes before the train's departure he returned to the station and jumped onto the train just as it was beginning to pull out of the station. A lady passenger, the only other person in his compartment, wondered where he had suddenly come from.

'Oh, you must be the one the militia were looking for!' she said.
'Yes, could be,' Jānis replied.

During the German occupation Jānis was inducted into the Latvian legion and by a miracle survived. As the German army retreated from Russia into Latvia he suffered from appendicitis and was operated on in Rīga. Before the Russians arrived he was transferred to a German Red Cross ship together with his wife, Genoveva and son, Roberts. Another son, Andris was born on the ship and upon arrival in Germany, Jānis quickly found his way to the American army to surrender. After he was released from a prisoner of war camp he bought an old yacht in England and, with a further addition to the family of a little girl named Māra, sailed first to Algeria and then across the Atlantic ocean via the Canary Islands to Trinidad in 26 days and four hours. Working on American ships as a captain, he was eventually able to immigrate with his family to Texas.

Back on the train, the Lejiņš family settled down for the long trip to Jelgava. There was not one Russian soul in sight! In our compartment there was only one other passenger, an old grandmother. She told us that the Germans had declared war on the Russians. We could hardly believe our ears! Teddy warned us not to speak too loudly, as we could be arrested for spreading rumors. The granny was startled by this, but then continued with renewed vigor, saying that she knew this for sure because her son had run home from work at noon and shouted that everybody had been told that war had broken out.

When we arrived in Jelgava we took a horse drawn taxi. As we drove across the Lielupe River the driver turned his head toward us and said just three words.
'War has begun!'
Every Latvian knew what these three words meant – it was the only way out from the Stalin nightmare. Teddy was doubtful.
'Who said that?' he asked.

'Everybody says so!' the driver replied.
Teddy was still not convinced.

There was the joy of reunion at my parents' farm, *Viesturi* and tears for our deported loved ones. Skaidrīte and her husband Konstantīns Gaters, nicknamed Kocis, came running home from work in Jelgava.
'War! War has begun!' they excitedly shouted from a distance.
But Teddy demanded to know whether they had heard an official announcement on the radio with their own ears? No, they hadn't, but...

That would not do for my husband. My father huddled by the radio and listened with his ear pressed against it. I unpacked everything and made beds for Teddy and I and the children in the room above the veranda. Everything was so clean and beautiful even though we had to sleep on sacks filled with hay instead of proper mattresses. A vase of fresh flowers from my mother's garden spread their scent and there was perfect peace in the house and wide open fields all around. Further away the woods began, and beyond the fields on that side of the property the Lielupe River flowed majestically by. On the far bank was a Russian airfield full of Russian war planes. From the window on the second floor you could see everything as if it was under a magnifying glass.

Kocis' parents were also deported and he was almost taken. Under interrogation by the Communists, Kocis was able to convince the officers that he wasn't himself, but rather his cousin.

Ina and Paulis' son, Imants hopped down the stairs and ran around the front of the veranda. At the "servants' end" of the house all the windows were wide open and the room was empty – precisely as it had been in that awful dream. Here, not so long ago, Vitauts and Austra's daughters, Inta and Dzintra had been running about with our Ina. Ina was still here, but where were Vitauts, Austra, and their little girls? Where were they?

Every summer all our relatives and friends descended from all over Latvia to the Irbe family farm, *Viesturi*. It was here where Aivars had been christened, and also here where the reverend Kārlis Irbe had married the army officer, Kocis to my sister, Skaidrīte.

Where were all our relatives and friends now? Where were Kārlis Irbe and the Kalniņš boys?

Are you all still alive, I wondered. I still feel you are here.

Chapter 5

The Second War: the loss of a child

One night we were discussing our future prospects over dinner. The children were asleep and the sun had set but the edge of the sky was still light from the fiery red glow of the sunset as is usual around Midsummer. Suddenly the sound of exploding bombs ripped through the air! We all ran up the stairs to my parent's bedroom. Through the window we saw, as if on a movie screen, one German bomber after another with their trapdoors open under their bellies and long bombs falling out and hitting the ground and exploding. I remembered the children, ran down stairs, grabbed them and crouched under the wooden staircase. The airfield was burning – all the Russian planes had been destroyed in a very short time. The German bombers departed.

I vomited and got diarrhea from the fright. I emptied myself completely! My mother made me drink hot wormwood tea. I was amazed that I could drink such an awful, bitter drink in one go – once the glass was empty I became completely calm. My husband poked fun at me, wanting to know what had happened to the heroine who was all set to shoot the two armed Russian soldiers back in Gulbene who had been threatening to deport us?

The Germans began bombarding Jelgava. I insisted that Ēriks, the oldest horse, be hitched to the cart and that we should all decamp to the forest. I heard objections from everybody.

'But the Germans will not bomb houses!'

'That may be, but what can one know for sure about the Germans?' I retorted.

So into the forest we all went. Teddy unhitched Ēriks and walked him to and fro alongside us, while the rest of us hid beneath the cart. Suddenly bomb shrapnel started raining down on us from all sides. It became positively dangerous. We jumped back into the cart and returned to the house, where we stayed another three years.

Skaidrīte and Kocis left to take over the running of Kocis' parents' farm which was being looked after by the farm hands after Kocis' parents were deported. Minister Kārlis Irbe turned up at *Viesturi* and hid himself with us. His family was somewhere out in the countryside but he didn't know for sure what had happened to them. Then one day my husband was chopping wood and saw coming down the lane towards him two German soldiers with SS letters on their shoulders. He went to meet them, still holding the axe in his hand and woke up to his mistake only when the soldiers lifted their rifles and aimed at him. The axe landed quickly enough in the bushes and then the soldiers asked him if any Russians were hiding in the vicinity?

'Nein!' Teddy replied.

They beamed when they heard he could speak German and accepted his invitation to come to the house and sit on the veranda, where there were windows all around - from three sides they could see everything. We offered them *Birkenwasser* (birch tree juice) but they politely declined. That sort of *Birkenwasser* is only used to massage into your hair they said. Apparently they took us for barbarians. Uncle Kārlis Irbe uncorked a bottle, and he and Teddy downed the cool clear liquid to the very last drop. The soldiers carefully took a sip and – right away– begged for more.

'It's like champagne!' they exclaimed.

Did they drink! Ina would not rest until she sat in the lap of one of the soldiers. He relented, took her up and began to tell us about his family.

Later Teddy got a job in Rīga, at the Dundaga Starch and Syrup Factory as an accountant. After reading his paper on Dialectic Materialism in Gulbene he had earned enemies and the school board had dismissed him from his teaching post. What would have happened to him if he had refused to give the lecture? The head of the Trade and Commercial School in Tukums offered him a job but it was too far from *Viesturi*.

On the weekends he rode his bicycle home from Rīga and helped with the farm work. There were no farm hands left on my parent's farm but the Germans had given them one Russian prisoner of war to be put to work. He was suffering from "an internal ailment". He worked a bit, then went off to "take care of business", then took a spade, looked up at the sky, and sang. My mother got fed up with him and exchanged him for another.

Timofei, the new replacement, was a sturdy chap. When he saw me, he eyed me a good while, then turned around swiftly and quickly got down to work. Timofei loved to eat bread; every time he cut himself a big, thick slice my mother sighed and said he was piercing her heart with a knife. When I kneaded dough at midnight for the week's supply of bread Timofei came into the kitchen several times to get a drink. I was sweating and was wearing a big apron and a kerchief on my head. He drank quickly, eyed me again, and then hurried back to his room. When we drove to Jelgava he confessed that he couldn't understand how Eduard Ivanovich[15] could live so long (five days) without his wife.

'It's not right,' he said, shaking his head.
I reflected – we have a professor here!

During Christmas and Easter a Russian refugee and her two children came and helped us with the work. Timofei came to life and began to work like mad! He built a bed for her and her children, otherwise they would have had to sleep on the floor, on hay, in the pirts (sauna). Sometimes he would lift some of the better morsels of food from our kitchen and give them to her. She was as happy as could be and went out of her way to please me. She liked the bed but complained that Timofei now insisted on sleeping in it with her. She, on the other hand, was equally adamant that she did not want to bring children into this world from just any passer-by.

---

15 Russians address men and women by their first name followed by their father's first name. Eduards father's name was Jānis (John), which in Russian is Ivan. Hence Eduard Ivanovich, meaning Eduard, son of John.

Poor Timofei, he was down in the dumps. He begged us to let him go on Saturday evenings to talk with his comrade on another farm. This was against German army regulations, but my mother let him go. After the first evening he returned home drunk, actually, completely sick. He was blind for three days running from the *samogonka* (moonshine) they had brewed. I had to clean the barn then and my mother had to milk the cows but when she got a headache from all the trouble I had to milk them, which I wasn't good at.

Timofei once confessed to me that after one of his hangover bouts, when my mother had scolded him, he was ready to drive a pitchfork into her when she had her back to him. But then he remembered us and broke out of his stupor. He respected my husband hugely and always wanted to talk about philosophy with me. One day he told me that there were a lot of mushrooms in the forest and that we should go and pick them for dinner.

'With you! Alone in the woods! Never!' I said.

He was taken aback and scratched his head.

'You're right,' he said after a while.

Laughing and shaking his head he grabbed a bucket and ran off to the forest.

Poor Timofei! He was forever dreaming about his wife and five kids back in Russia. He had never loved her so much as now he often said.

Teddy had to go to Rīga to fetch Aivars' bed from Teddy's mother's house. Timofei accompanied him, though this was also strictly forbidden. He donned my husband's good coat and proudly and happily sat with him in the driver's seat of the cart. He returned home unusually silent. One day I was washing a window on the upper floor while Timofei was digging in the garden below. Abruptly he threw down his spade and called up to me saying that it was all lies about us being poor because in reality we were capitalists! I shouted back that while we were able to get by we were by no means rich. We lived on our teachers' wages and all the "expensive" furniture he had seen in my husband's mother's house we had bought on credit. Her house did not belong to us either and this house had also been bought on credit by my parents, and also only from their teachers' salaries. We were "poor" because the German rations were meager and everything had to be bartered for, since nobody could eat money. Timofei began to laugh – now he understood. He became a little more settled, gained weight and learned Latvian from Ina - every Sunday he learnt his language lesson by heart that she had assigned him.

Ina, in turn, learned Russian from him, and learned German and primary school subjects from her grandfather. Furthermore she had devised her own alphabet so that we couldn't read her diary. She learned musical notes from me: I wrote their names on the piano keys – *do, re, mi, fa, sol, la, ti, do.* After a couple of years she took us by surprise by playing the *Melancholy Waltz*, the most popular piece composed by the renowned Latvian composer, Emīls Dārziņš.

Since we didn't intend to return to Gulbene it was time to go and fetch the furniture we had left there. I went to the Jelgava railway station and asked the station master, a German, if we could have a wagon allocated to us on the train from Gulbene so we could collect our belongings. I explained that I was pregnant and my children were lacking clothing and beds. At the same time I presented him with a bouquet of roses from my parent's garden. I got it! He gave me a copy of the letter he was sending to the station master in Gulbene. A whole wagon!

Winter came. I rode from Rīga to Gulbene in a lorry. It snowed sporadically along the way. When I finally arrived in Gulbene it was already freezing and our old apartment was forbiddingly cold. The wood in the shed had not been chopped. I fell asleep, fully dressed, in my fur coat, mittens and boots with several thick blankets on top of me and the carpet to boot! The next day Alvīna arrived, chopped some wood, and got the fire going. Miss Apse also turned up and asked if she could help. I declined her services. She left us, but there was a peculiar air about her.

Alvīna went off to the countryside armed with good vodka and tobacco which Teddy had acquired in exchange for syrup. She soon came back with her friends who loaded all our furniture into their horse carriages. They even loaded the spare fire wood into the carriages and then transferred everything into the designated freight train wagon which was waiting at the railway station. During this time I went to say goodbye to everyone at the school. I shook hands with the director, the same man who had written to my husband, *"Due to unfortunate circumstances you can no longer be employed at the school"*. I pretended I knew nothing about the letter.

'It's a pity we can't work here anymore. It's too far from our parents in these trying times, when Latvians are denouncing Latvians. We were offered jobs in Tukums but we declined.'
He smiled uncomfortably when I said 'Thank you' a second time.

I returned to Rīga in another lorry, stiff from the cold. I was taken to Jelgava by my friend, Ēriks, my parents' faithful horse. Snow drifts covered the road here and there, and in between shone the slippery asphalt. It was hard for Ēriks and I let him take his own stride. I sat huddled in my fur coat, turning into ice, despite pulling a big shawl around me and digging my winter boots under a thick layer of hay. It was a sparsely populated 40 kilometers from Rīga to Jelgava. I had begun my journey from Gulbene at dawn and arrived back at *Viesturi* after midnight. My mother ran out to meet me overcome with anguish; there were famished escaped Russian prisoners of war hiding in the nearby forest.

Teddy was interrogated by the police on account of that lecture on dialectical materialism and released. The charges were dropped. In 1942 I had been carrying little Atis already for five months under my heart and was surprised when I received a summons to appear at the German secret police office in Rīga. The officer, a Latvian, got up when I was admitted and smiling, politely offered me a chair.

'Has your husband received money from the communists?' he asked.
'No!'

'Why did he give a lecture on dialectic materialism?'

'He had to do what the school board asked him to do. Somebody had to do it if the party said so.'

'Were you given a holiday in the Crimea?'

'Goodness no!' I exclaimed, surprised.

'Do you admire Lenin?'

'No! Whose been telling you all this?'

'Well, think a bit!'

My brain started to race.

'Don't tell me it was Miss Apse!'

'The same,' he laughed. 'I never took this case seriously but we have our regulations and in my job I am obliged to observe them.'

He rose and shook my hand.

'I feel very relieved that you are not a nervous woman. Your husband came here earlier and thoroughly frightened me! Goodbye!'

Aivars became capricious in the evenings before bedtime. I wondered why he now always held his head backwards and cried. Once he fell backwards three times in a row from his chair. I stood with little Aivars on the highway with a piece of bacon and some eggs, begging the lorry drivers to take us to the hospital in Rīga in exchange for the food. A bone specialist, who had managed to save a very good x-ray machine, received us. The pictures showed that Aivars had contracted TB in two discs of his backbone. Then I had to take him to the Rīga Tuberculosis hospital, from where, after two months, he would be transferred to the Krimulda sanatorium in Sigulda, some forty kilometers from Rīga. There was no horse cabby anywhere so I had to carry Aivars on my back even though I was carrying six month old Atis under my heart. I put Aivars down and let him walk, dragging his little wooden horse on wheels behind him. Abruptly he stopped in the middle of the road.

'You can shoot me, but I cannot walk anymore!' he shouted.

I left him in the hospital. It was a painful parting for both of us.

In addition to the dream I had in Gulbene I also had other dreams:

Dream No. 2. When we arrived in *Viesturi* from Gulbene on June 22, I saw in my dream that night a huge herd of sheep against a blazing sunset, being chased across the sky by giant, bushy, galloping horses with huge, powerful chests and flaring nostrils. Upon awakening I thought that it was a sign that the Germans would drive out the Russians. This soon enough turned out to be true.

Dream No. 3. When the German army drove the Russians out of Rīga on July 1, I had a dream that night about a swarm of huge, green grasshoppers covering the whole sky and approaching *Viesturi*. I hid in a ditch by the cemetery in the forest. But then the grasshoppers turned into Russian pilots who jumped out of their green aeroplanes and with revolvers in their hands began running towards our house. How could I warn my loved ones to flee? I awoke. I saw it as a sign that the Russians would come back. My father was the only one who agreed with me and believed in my dreams.

Dream No. 4. From the direction of Jelgava, across the Lielupe River, a grey rider galloped across the sky, throwing grenades in all directions. I hid myself next to the potato heap. This time my father said that the dream was wrong, because the Russians could not come from Jelgava, from the south.

Father was wrong. The Russians surprised the German army and pushed into the middle of Latvia from Lithuania, taking Jelgava on July 31, 1944. Rīga was only freed from the Germans three months later, on October 13, at the very same time that the Soviet army took Eastern Prussia, thereby cutting off the German army's escape route over land, back to Germany.

I knew if the dream came true I would never see Aivars again. I hurried to the Jelgava station. I was now eight months pregnant, still I was not allowed onto the train to Rīga. It was a munitions train. I approached the first wagon which was filled with German soldiers. I told them in my broken German my story – and they pulled me inside! They were polite and started a conversation with me and I did my best to contribute my bit as best I could. Time flew as we talked. We chugged through Rīga and reached Sigulda where they lifted me down onto the platform. Apparently Germans have warm feelings about expectant mothers, but it never occurred to me one bit that something terrible could have happened to me traveling in a munitions train, hidden among soldiers on the way to the front. I returned in the same way, but this time in a train empty of munitions.

In Sigulda I took the shortest way to the Krimulda sanatorium, crawling up the steep bank of the Gauja River. I was permitted to stay there for three days and became acquainted with conditions there. I slept in the attic, a little room where the seamstress mended sheets and other things. The hapless children slept in the sun, bathed in sweat and their own urine. They were thirsty but there was only one nurse to take care of them all. I told the director that I wanted to take Aivars home.

'Certainly. I am driving home in my car for a holiday very soon. *Viesturi* is not so far from my parish. I'll bring Aivars with me.'

The day arrived. We couldn't hold back our feelings, waiting at *Viesturi*. Aivars was carried out of a black car. His back was strapped to a sand bag on a board with cloth straps so that his back remained rigid. My father, mother, grandfather and I all burst out crying. Timofei was battling bravely to hold his tears back and couldn't stop shaking his head. We were all overjoyed!

Aivars was put in a sunny room upstairs which had a window and a door leading out onto the balcony above the veranda. The sand bag on his back was heavy, but nevertheless in good weather we carried him onto the balcony so that he could sleep in the fresh air and sunbathe. This way, just by turning his head, he could see the forest, fields and a little bit of the Lielupe river. After half a year I started to put him down on his stomach and later, still strapped to the board, Timofei carried him down to sleep in front of the house. Once Aivars pleaded with me to let him feel the trunk of a tree, he wanted to know how strong it was. I let him crawl with the board tied to his back and was amazed how agile he was! He reached the tree in no time and embraced it – a look of pure happiness broke out all over his little face! I cried.

One day I heard him pounding away with a hammer.
 'Aivars is at it again!' I exclaimed.
 'I keep giving him all the rusty nails I can find. I wonder where he puts them,' Ina said.

Then I heard another noise. I climbed up the stairs and opened the door. Aivars was a little afraid and red in the face. He looked at me with a sideways glance as he kicked his feet against the sand bag. Everything seemed to be in order, the straps were in place. I went back down the stairs.

Then I heard the noise again. This time I climbed the stairs very quietly so they didn't squeak and quickly threw open the door. My dear little son had pushed his heavy bed half way across the room – crawling! Behind his bed he had driven the nails into the wall in a cluster and closer to the end of the bed was a gaping hole.
 'Why did you make such a big hole in the wall?'
 'I wanted to see what was on the other side.'
I decided to carry him more often into the garden and let him crawl around there. The neighbors said Aivars would be an opera star.
 'When he shouts "Mamma…" the whole neighborhood can hear him.'

Teddy was away in Rīga. My father was holding the reins and I was sitting next to him, in pain, as Ēriks galloped along the cobblestoned streets of Jelgava. There was a full moon that night and I was watching the back of Ēriks' hoofs. His hoof-beats echoed hollow in the moonlit night and occasionally sparks flew as his hoofs pounded the stones. Arriving at the hospital, I immediately asked where the operating room was. The nurse said that she should first get me ready but I replied that it was time and that I was clean. I had hardly reached the table when out came Atis. He was the only one of our children with dark hair. He ate very little. I had to feed him every three hours and therefore had to stay in hospital for three days. Teddy arrived and handed me a poem he had composed for the occasion. What beautiful feelings he had expressed in it for me and our new son. I cried with joy. Teddy took our son in his strong arms but Atis, yawning widely, immediately fell asleep. Back home we were all gathered together once again. If only it could have lasted forever!

A representative from our school in Venspils arrived and asked us to sign a petition begging the Germans to spare the school's doctor, a Jew. There were only two doctors in Ventspils, the other one was German. But our school's doctor, Dr. Feitelbergs had begun his practice way before the First World War and was held in high esteem by everybody. We signed the petition, even though it could have put us in danger. Alas, the many collected signatures did not help. Later we heard a rumor that Dr. Feitelbergs and both his sons were shot in a Ventspils meadow.

We nicknamed Ina the "village broom". She was constantly on the move, running off to wash and dress the professor's kids on his small farm, then off to see the old woman, Liepa who lived by the forest. Without my noticing, she always changed little Atis' diapers. When he cried, she sang folksongs to him until he fell asleep. Skaidrīte and her son, Jānis paid us a visit after New Year's. We put Atis at one end of the bed and Jānis at the other and waited to see what they would do. They observed one another and then, as if they had arranged it previously, both started to shriek simultaneously.

Ina went to the Darta primary school in Jelgava. She got top grades in everything. She was a strong girl. Her favorite activity was riding her bike. But after three months back at school she again became forgetful, just as she had in Gulbene. We took her out of school. Then she became sick in the beginning of 1943. The winter grew ever colder, and the stoves couldn't heat up the house enough – the wind howled through the chimney and the pipes on the stoves. Ina's temperature climbed. I watched her – how beautiful she looked! I put warm compresses around her ears, and then forgot myself. Suddenly I saw a small white coffin being taken into the cellar – I couldn't have dreamed that! Ina opened her eyes at once.

'Mommy, will I die?' she asked.

I was gripped with fear, but I replied, 'No dearest Ina, you will become well again.'

Then one day in January she said, 'Mommy, if I don't go to school now, I will never go to school.'

So we put her back in school. Her ears were fine, but during a visit to the doctor she fainted when the doctor tested her ears. The teacher at school also informed us that she fainted during morning prayer. She no longer had any appetite. She was merry though and danced for Aivars, and he laughed.

'Her eyes are as big as two lanterns,' a Jewish woman told me after she stopped us on the street in Jelgava.

The others in our household couldn't see what I could see. I was on standby all the time.

'Ina, my little one, I won't let you go to school anymore – unless you eat more!'

'What's the use Mommy, nothing I eat stays down. And I don't want to go to school either.'

I took her to the hospital. The doctors were at a loss. They punctured her ear drums but no puss appeared. They took out her appendix. On the third day she was standing by the window, waiting for her grandfather to come and fetch her and again, she fainted. She stayed at the hospital. The next day I arrived. The nurse complained that Ina wanted to pee all the time, and she was forever running to give her a pot. But she was the only nurse on duty. I told the doctor, a young man, that Ina needed to pee all the time and he promised to stay with his "beautiful little bride" day and night.

Ina was smiling again, she was happy. As I went to leave she threw her arms around my neck.

'Mommy you better make a coffin for me. I'm hurting,' she said.
'Please, my little girl, don't speak like that. It hurts me very much.'
'All right, Mommy.'
They were to be her last words to me.

Returning home everybody questioned me with their eyes.
'All is well,' I answered.
Night descended. Everybody was sleeping. My agonizing thoughts
were with her. Abruptly the door opened and Ina stretched out her arms.
'Mommy! Mommy!' she shouted.
'Dearest Ina, are you here already?' I asked in wonder as I put my
legs over the edge of the bed.

It was still dark. I looked at the clock – three in the morning. I got
dressed and went down to the kitchen to cook the meals for the boys and
the rest of the family for the day. Then I tidied myself for the trip back
to the hospital. My mother rose at six to milk the cow.
'Are you up already?'
'I will get Timofei to harness the horse. I'm going to the hospital.'
Just then somebody knocked on the door. It was our neighbor.
'The hospital is on the telephone…'

I arrived and found Ina's bed empty.
'Did my Ina call out for me?' I asked the person in the bed next to hers.
'Yes!'
'When?'
'Around three.'

I found Ina. Her kidneys had been operated on, it was thought they were
not working. Urine poisoning. I called the nurse and insisted she put Ina
in a warm bath. She did my biding immediately. Ina was asleep. She
opened her eyes, closed them, then yawned. The doctor put her under a
glass cupola to keep her warm. There was no other apparatus. I held her
hand, which moved a little, now and then. I didn't pray to God because I
knew my little girl would die. She yawned again, then opened her eyes,

but they were no longer seeing anything. I remembered I had seen the same look in Mudīte's eyes, Vitauts and Austra's daughter, just before she died. I sat next to her and suddenly noticed that her eyes had lost focus altogether. She died from a brain infection.

I was there all alone, my little Ina was no more. The doctor took me to his room and gave me something to swallow. Then I was no more. When I awoke, the doctor questioned me in detail about Ina's possible ailments. Only then did I recall her fall down the stairs from the second floor when she was six months old. Maybe something had been dislodged in her brain? The doctors in Latvia did not do brain operations. Her appendix and kidneys were in perfect condition.

I returned home and once again the family questioned me with their eyes. I wanted to speak, but couldn't.
'Ina is no more,' I finally brought myself to whisper.
Grandfather Jānis cried, clutching his head in his hands, bemoaning why God hadn't taken him in Ina's place? My father stammered short, anguished cries.
'My beloved and only little friend – Inochka!' Timofei wailed without end.

With tear laden eyes my mother and I did the housework in silence. Teddy arrived from Rīga.
'Speak, Punktiņ. Speak! Our little girl didn't mean that we should perish!'

We traveled to Jelgava to dress our daughter. She was lying naked. Have they no shame! How cruel can people be! While Teddy went to get a white coffin I dressed my cold little girl. A strange, warm feeling came over me, it seemed that it also flowed into Ina. Lightly, caressingly, I lifted her arms, her body. She was so light, so trusting of me. Somebody asked Teddy who the coffin was for.
'It's for Ina.'
The man was left standing speechless and none the wiser.

At home everybody was weaving wreaths in silence. Only my Grandfather Jānis was talking to his seven month old great grandson, Atis, bouncing him on his lap. I glanced through the veranda window and saw my husband bringing the horse into the yard with the white coffin in the cart – precisely as I had seen in my vision.

The funeral was held on April 8, 1943. Relatives, friends and the teachers and students from the Darta primary school arrived. The female pupils looked towards Ina's body in trepidation.

'Did she look like that? She seems completely different,' they said.

I observed my Ina. Something had happened! It seemed that her forehead had partly sunken in on one side, under the skin, her scull had collapsed. I was not allowed to look at her anymore – it all seemed like a dream. The guests were amazed that I could speak to them politely and care for them. Then the time arrived when we had to say goodbye to Ina. I begged for the lid not to be put on yet and went out to find some violets, my parting gift for my little girl. Why was everybody staring at me? My husband took me by the arm.

'We will follow the coffin – collect yourself!' he said.

The cemetery was right by the edge of the forest. The school choir sang and its orchestra played. I observed a yellow butterfly fluttering among the flowers placed on the grave. Teddy was holding me tightly in his arms and I was holding him tightly. Only the two of us were left, with the little grave, and the butterfly above it... Even to this day, whenever we quarrel and we look for who is to blame, I remember this sight and feel that we are still holding on tightly to each other. This has guided me safely throughout our entwined lives.

In my dreams I was continually searching for my little girl. I was in a tram in Rīga traveling along the Daugava River and Ina was next to me. Suddenly she disappeared. I ran to look in the next tram that arrived – empty. In the next – again empty. I ran along the bank of the river. A chest of drawers stood on the bank. I pulled open the top drawer – and saw Ina lying in it. Across the Daugava the sun was shining brightly and the ice was glittering. On the other side there were hills, one after the other, covered with trees. I knew I had to search there for my Ina. But there was a strong current flowing in the middle of the river. Would I be able to cross the river and climb all those hills? I dropped to my knees on the ice and begged God to give my Ina back to me.

Little Atis was learning to sit and stand all by himself. He no longer had his sister to help and amuse him. His fingers were strong. There was no sign of the disease which he had picked up in the hospital after his birth. A week after we arrived home we had to return to the hospital. He had a boil on almost every finger. They had to be cut and the puss and blood squeezed out. We stayed in the hospital for three more days. I learned how to dress his fingers and then returned home. At the hospital many of the babies had the runs and other sicknesses, we just couldn't remain there. Miraculously no more boils appeared.

Atis was crawling around in Aivars' room. He had to give his toys to his big brother all the time, and he readily did this. But Aivars wouldn't give them back! There was nothing left for Atis to do other than lift his face up to the sky and cry full throttle. However, when he was in his Grandfather Kristaps' lap he was quiet and could sit for hours observing my father as he read his newspaper. But my father had to leave us. My sister's husband, Kocis Gaters had joined the Latvian Legion as an officer and had gone off to the eastern front. He couldn't come to terms with the deportation of his parents by the Russians during the *Year of Terror*. Thus, my sister, Skaidrīte and my father went to work the land on the Gaters' big farm by themselves.

Once Atis disappeared, as Aivars had done earlier. When we had only recently arrived at *Viesturi*, Aivars used to crawl about and pretend to eat the grass. He was imitating Ēriks and, just like Ēriks, he would shake his head to drive the flies away. Suddenly he was nowhere to be seen. Teddy got angry that so many women couldn't look after one child!

And we women, were scared and at our wits' end, feeling guilty. I ran along the potato field watching alertly – what was that? At one end of a furlough the potato tops appeared to be moving forward and then in the next furlough they were starting to move again but in the opposite direction. I waited until the movement stopped at my end. Then out crawled Aivars! His face was so black that I could only see his eyes!

One day Atis was nowhere to be seen. His pram was in the garden but it was empty. I searched inside the house twice then rushed back out into the garden. Then I saw him! He was dangling, head first, from the pram, on the side facing the house and playing with the pebbles on the ground. I had tied him into the pram. The little boy had lurched over the side and remained hanging by the straps.

In the middle of summer I regained my speech. I hadn't been able to speak for three months after Ina's death. Dumb and silent I went about my chores. My mother was constantly opening the bedroom door and sticking her head in to check if I had fed Atis and to make sure I had not dropped him on the floor as I put him to bed. I lost my memory for a long time. I broke dishes while washing them because my hands went in a different direction than I wanted them to go.

'It doesn't matter. When we have to flee from the Russians we won't be able to take them with us anyway,' I said.

I was convinced the Germans were lying and that they were not preparing any 'sack' to catch the Russians. I had everything ready to take with us. In the linen towel my mother had given us as a gift I had sewn in a number of pockets where I could store oat meal, rice (in case anybody should contract the runs), manna and other staples. The towel could then be thrown over the shoulder and this way both hands would be free. The Germans had already taken Timofei and my mother had given him a lot of food but he didn't believe he would come back. He said that he would distribute the food to his friends and refused to take my husband's good coat. He was convinced that the Germans would take it from him. He left us looking very worried.

Little Aija came into this world very easily in the summer of 1944. Just the previous evening I had walked to the cemetery with scissors to crop the grass around Ina's beautiful little grave around which Timofei had planted small evergreen shrubs. Next to her lay my grandfather, Jānis Jostsons, who died not long after Ina. I had never seen him sick. I can still see him sitting in the yard on a block of wood. The hens walked about on his shoulders and even hopped on his head. He was ninety-three years old.

I fetched water from the well to water Ina's flowers. Thinking about her I suddenly felt her walking beside me, her warm hand in mine... only for a fleeting moment but long enough to make me believe that miracles can happen. There is another life – a spiritual life. Our hearts will stop beating one day but there is also our soul.

That night I had only just laid down in bed when I heard somebody crossing over our little bridge. Teddy had arrived from Rīga! Around five in the morning I started getting pains. What luck! Teddy was there to help me in my hour of need!

'Get up!' I shouted to Teddy.

Ēriks had pneumonia, so Teddy ran over to the Liepa's farm and fetched their horse but he was too wide for our harness. I hurried Teddy along, and he got nervous, as my mother already was. The little ones were still sound asleep. Finally we got the horse harnessed and away we galloped. In the middle of the bridge across the Lielupe river, leading to Jelgava, the harness dropped off the horse. A few travelers went past but no-one had a rope or strap. Teddy pulled off the leather belt from his trousers and somehow managed to attach the harness to the horse. My water had already broken. We only had to gallop a little bit more before we arrived at the hospital which was by the railway station. I threw myself onto the operating table as the nurses shouted at me not to let go – but I couldn't wait! Aija came out at that very moment.

'Is it a girl?' I asked.

'Yes!'

Ina, my dearest, had come back to me! My mother said Aija's little nose was as small as that of a little bird.

The air raid siren started wailing in the night. I grabbed Aija and dashed across the park to an air raid shelter. I was one of the first to arrive. Other mothers stayed in the hospital. In the morning my lungs went on strike. I couldn't catch my breath. The nurse put mustard bandages on my back but that didn't help.

'See what you have done! Why did you sit on the bed by an open window in a draft and braid your hair?' the doctor scolded me.

I remembered that after Ina's death I fell sick with a lung infection. I had accompanied Teddy for a while across our little bridge in a thin blouse on a windy day. That night I felt as if somebody was stabbing me in the back with a knife. That was the first time Ina appeared to me in my dreams. She came up to my bed and put her hand on my back. I was so happy I wanted to embrace her, but she pulled back abruptly and ran away. I sweated without end but still during the day went to help my mother with her chores as we were the only ones left on the farm and she was already working above her limits.

The next night at the hospital the siren started again and once again I ran to the shelter. My lungs worked perfectly. But as soon as I was back in bed I began to choke again. The doctor was of the opinion that this was from heightened nervousness, the result of my nervous breakdown after Ina's death. He said it would be better if I returned home. And so I did.

I said goodbye to the Russian woman who was in the bed next to mine. Hardly anybody paid any attention to her because she didn't know Latvian and while she was in jail had got pregnant to a German. I took pity on her because she had suffered so much. I asked the nurse to give me what I needed and then I passed it on to the Russian. I bid farewell to the other women, the nurses and the doctor. Teddy came to fetch us. He looked attractive, dressed in a white shirt and bronzed by the sun. He worked every evening at *Viesturi*, helping to harvest the hay, carrying mountains of dried grass on his pitchfork. He was strong and muscular. But how did I look!

The neighbors arrived to pay their respects to me and the new baby, Aija. Everybody was delighted. I put Aivars in the garden to let him crawl and feel everything with his hands. Ēriks was fit once more and Teddy returned to Rīga. I stared in amazement at the sky and wondered what was exploding so high up? No aeroplanes could be seen anywhere. Were they bombs that hadn't reached the earth? I saw a woman running by the wheat field. Bullets whizzed by her and she jumped into the wheat to hide. From then on we slept in the underground bunker that was covered by earth. During the day we continued to work. An elderly woman came to us and begged us for shelter. She became a "granny" to us and cooked the food while my mother took care of the farm and milked the cows. I looked after the children.

We were told that we should heat the stove everyday so that smoke rose from the chimney day and night because the Germans were burning empty houses during the night. We watched as the people commandeered by the German army to dig trenches near our farm scatter in all directions. They must have run away. Nobody kept cattle in the barns anymore. Our bunker was now full of people and I slept with my children on straw in the second section. The older women fed us and gave us drinks. I felt anger towards the single women who never came to help. Outside the raspberries were ripe and as big as thumbs and juicy plumbs were vying for space on the branches of the plumb trees. Such an over abundance of berries and nobody was picking them! Stealthily I left the bunker and started to crawl towards the berry bushes to pick berries for my children. I didn't hear the shots but bullets slammed themselves behind my feet into the dirt. Not far from the boundary of our farm was a big ditch lined with trees. Apparently they were shooting from there. I decided not to risk my life anymore and returned to the bunker.

Eight days after I returned home from hospital I had another dream. Paulis, one of the Kalniņš boys who was tortured to death by the KGB ran into our kitchen. His face and his light blue police uniform were covered with blood.

'Anna, why are you still here! Jelgava is burning!'
I ran into the storeroom, grabbed our big rye bread sack, spied our salt bag on the floor, grabbed that too, and ran to my children. In the morning I couldn't fathom whether I dreamed it all or whether it really happened. I got up and glanced out the window – Jelgava was in flames! And the bridge across the Lielupe river had been destroyed.

I waited for Teddy. He came racing from Rīga on a bicycle. Aija was ten days old.

'Why are you still here?'
'Well, there was some kind of shooting. We didn't dare venture outside.'

He immediately harnessed Ēriks. I had all the necessary things packed already. I regretted having to leave the big crystal bowl with the golden inscription which we got for our wedding. I couldn't stop myself from snatching the stainless steel knives, forks and spoons. My mother heaved a huge lump of bacon and other foodstuffs into the cart. But then the professor from the farm next door came running with his wife and children. He no longer had a horse and pleaded with us to take them with us. We had to throw out our sacks of food so his kids could fit in the cart. He said that his brother had a farm near Rīga and he would be able to replace the food we had to leave behind. However, I kept my packed provisions and a rather big chunk of the bacon, which my mother handed to me when nobody was looking. She didn't come with us because she had to feed the cattle. Teddy returned to fetch her later.

As we went past the cemetery I wanted to say farewell to my dearest Ina, but Teddy would not hear of it.

'We must think of those still living – Ina would understand that – and we have to hurry!'

By the gates of the cemetery, with their backs against the wall, two Latvian legionaries sat chomping on sandwiches.

'What are you doing here?' we asked.

'There's no army left. Everything is helter-skelter. We're just resting.'

The adults walked alongside the cart. I looked after the children in the cart and sometimes got out and walked when somebody wanted to rest their feet and take my place in the cart for a while.

The farm house Viesturi

Ina in 1943 her last year

Viesturi in 1944. Kristaps and son Jānis in 1944
with Eriks, the faithful horse

Chapter six.

Flight

Thus, ten months before the end of the war we began our refugee journey. Dusk was already setting when we neared Rīga. As we drove across the iron bridge that spans the Daugava River we saw fiery explosions in the sky. We huddled closer together in the cart, but couldn't stop Ēriks from taking free rein. Air raid sirens commenced wailing as soon as we crossed the bridge. Never before had I seen Ēriks galloping so furiously – he must have taken fright! Not far from the University of Latvia we rushed into a bunker, in Vērmanītis Park. Teddy remained standing outside by a tree, consoling Ēriks. When we emerged from the bunker we saw that things had fallen on the ground from the sky, they looked like bomb fragments. We continued on our way towards Teddy's cousin, Hamilkars Lejiņš and his wife Zenta's, who lived in Mežparks. I can't remember when our neighbors from *Viesturi*, the professor and his family left us. I just remember that he promised to high heaven that he would compensate us for the food we threw out, but he disappeared without a trace.

When we arrived in Mežparks, Hamilkars and Zenta were packing in a frenzy to get on a boat the next day that was secretly heading for Sweden. But the boat didn't belong to them and it was already full of refugees. We were left stranded.

The next day we were left alone with Hamilkars' father and Zenta's mother. I picked a few berries for my children from the red currant bushes. Teddy diligently cleaned up after Ēriks, nevertheless Hamilkars' father complained that they would soon be left without any berries and that Ēriks had made the place stink. Zenta's mother overheard this and scolded him.

'Shame on you! Your own children are braving the sea in a small boat, we don't know what awaits them and you are behaving like a cad!'

Hamilkars' father immediately bent over baby Aija and kissed her, then he kissed Aivars and Atis.

'Please forgive me, my little children,' he begged.

The air raids continued unabated and we thought it best to move to our friend's place in the countryside, north of Rīga, in Vidzeme. But I was shocked when we arrived there that Melānija showed me and the kids to an unfinished attic as our next home. We picked our way gingerly across the sand that had been spread on the floor to a hay stack in the middle of an empty room. Half the window had a glass pane, the other half had cardboard nailed over it. I turned full circle and climbed down not saying a word. I put Aija on the floor in the study, then put Aivars next to her. Atis toddled after me – he was my best assistant already at two years of age. All I had to say was, 'Atis, hand me this or hand me that…' and he was there to help. Melānija watched me, not saying a word. When the children were bedded, I turned to her.

'Thank you. You are most gracious!' I said.

'You are welcome,' she replied.

So we stayed in one corner of the study. I made the food with Melānija and gave her stockings or underwear as payment in kind whenever I needed milk or eggs.

Sometime later, Teddy returned to *Viesturi* to fetch my mother. *Viesturi* was no more. The upper floor had been razed and the ground floor vandalized. The crystal bowl had disappeared and the piano was standing in the garden! A huge silence reigned over the desolation. No one at the Liepa's farm knew what had happened to my mother. Teddy began his return trek and as he passed the forester's house he saw a woman sitting on the edge of a well with her back to the road.

'May I water my horse here?' Teddy asked.

She turned her head – it was my mother! She cried with joy. They embraced and kissed each other and then quickly returned to *Viesturi*, where my mother had buried some of her belongings and sacks of food. She had a lot of clothes but Teddy wouldn't let her take them all. My father's wedding (or funeral) suit had to be left behind. They did, however, take one cow with them. It was a long journey back to Melānija's and they arrived very late and dead tired.

I cried frequently in the night. Why did people change so in times of hardship? We had to hear that our cow was eating all the grass and that there would be nothing left for their cow, even though my mother was careful to make sure our cow only ate grass from alongside the ditch. I felt very sorry for my mother. Then I got angry and gave the landlady a piece of my mind. I was frightened by my outburst. We decided that we had to return to Rīga anyway, because on this side of Rīga, in Vidzeme, the Russians were bound to come, sooner or later. We settled down at my brother, Paulis' house on Vējzaķu Island and there, on this bit of land, our little cow could feed herself to her heart's content and supply us with all the milk we needed.

One day Teddy said that we would have to discard a lot of the things we had taken with us. We needed to repack, keeping only the very essentials. Seized by an inner alarm he jumped on his bicycle and rode off to his former work place, the Dundaga starch factory. I tried to stop him because I feared the Germans would grab him and make him dig trenches. All the employees had already been evacuated to Liepāja but my husband still had the keys. No sooner had he entered his old office when the telephone rang. At the other end was Aivar's godmother, Elza. Her father had served in the Latvian secret police and had been tortured to death by the Russians. She told Teddy that the German officer who rented a flat from her was going to deliver a freight train to Germany. She and her two sons had already secured a place on the freight train, in a corner of one of the wagons. There was a little space next to hers which could accommodate us too!

My husband tore back home in no time and we grabbed our things in a frenzy. I put on my fur coat, wrapped the children in blankets and Teddy loaded us all into the cart. I had Aija in my arms, Atis on my lap and Aivars on my back with my mother hanging onto my right elbow. Ēriks took off at a fast trot with Teddy running alongside him, holding the reins. The sky opened up and it began to thunder and rain like cats and dogs. It was warm and humid. My strength had left me and I was amazed that my mother could still cling to me. We arrived at the railway station where we had to stop as Ēriks could not go over the rails with the cart. The wheels would break. Crouching, almost on all fours, we wove our way between the wagons of the train, I had the children, Teddy had our belongings. My mother stayed behind with Ēriks until we found our place in the train. After work my brother Paulis arrived and led Ēriks back to his house.

As it happened, we had panicked in vain. The freight train remained standing in the same place for a whole week. We were surrounded by other trains on all sides, some of which were full of refugees. Teddy dropped a hint to the German officer that an offer of a small bribe to the train drivers might help. Indeed, it did. The officer gave them a whole box of assorted alcoholic beverages and the drivers, finding themselves in a happy mood, took turns listening to a small radio to find out when the German army was going to push back the Russians from the Tukums railway station's shuttle yard. In this way we were shunted back and forth in the train for a day and a night until the next night, frightened out of our dreams, we felt that the train really was running! We left Rīga in the last days of September.

We traveled at speed the whole night in heightened apprehension. We feared that at one of the stations the doors would burst open and the men would be taken to dig trenches for the Germans. At the last moment the most dreadful thing could happen – the men folk could have been separated from their families. The morning arrived. The train stopped. Carefully we nudged the door open. I saw a sign, *Marienburg*. We were in Germany, in Eastern Prussia!

'We got out! We're free!' Teddy shouted with joy.

I couldn't speak. I remember seeing tears running down Elza's cheeks. She was sorry to have left her Motherland. I was sorry for nothing. All I could think about was would I be able to deliver my little children to safety?

In Marienburg Teddy bought us tickets to Berlin. Ēlza and her children accompanied us but I couldn't say a word, couldn't think anything. I had to rest my mind. Above everything else I needed inner quiet. In Berlin, Ēlza said goodbye to us and we, the five members of the Lejiņš family, and my mother remained standing on the railway platform. Teddy hurried off to buy tickets to Bad Schandau by the Elbe River, where his mother's sister was living. She was German, as was Teddy's mother. Suddenly – out of a clear blue sky – there was an air raid! The railway platform was deserted; we were the only ones on it. We crouched as tightly as possible next to our belongings and waited. The aeroplanes swarmed overhead as thick as a plague of grasshoppers. I began to count the bombers in the sky as I lay on the platform. Were they American? They flew over us and then disappeared. They didn't drop any bombs on us.

The train took us through Dresden. Bad Schandau was further up the Elbe river very close to the Czechoslovakian border. But we found we could not stay at Teddy's auntie's place. She only had two rooms in a building that had been turned over to German refugees. We quartered ourselves in a hotel room where the doors opened directly onto the Elbe river. The room was cold and damp, but, oh, the beds were wide and soft! And everything was so clean! Little Aija was already three months old and lived entirely on my milk. She seemed a little pale, perhaps she wasn't getting enough milk from me? She didn't cry and slept well. Just to be sure she was okay I took her to a doctor with Aivars on my back and Atis by my side. The doctor declared that Aija was slowly gaining weight and hence was alright. Every evening before we went to bed my mother ironed the damp bed sheets – then we were all warm, though everything around us, including the walls, was damp. The Hungarian cook allowed me to cook food for my children in the kitchen. I stretched the food out to also include my mother, Teddy and I.

The manageress of the hotel, however, kept running into our room to check what we were doing. She complained that we were burning up too much electricity.

'Are you doing any ironing?' she asked.

'Of course not!'

Our German marks were coming to an end. We got them in Latvia when Teddy sold our expensive and comfortable children's pram on the black market. Every day Teddy went out to look for work. He traveled to Sebnitz, not too far north of Bad Schandau, early every morning and took his place in the "employment line" at the town council building. He demanded work, pointing out that he had three small children and two adults to support, not including himself. He laid out all his papers on the table, including the ones that testified he had donated his fur coat to the German army in Latvia (i.e. the Latvian Legion) and that the Germans had requisitioned our copper candlesticks and food from the farm. He continued with this ritual from morning to evening every day for a week until the Mayor got tired of him and gave him a job in a factory warehouse sorting out machine parts.

We moved to Sebnitz where from the railway station we were taken by horse drawn wagon to our new, one room apartment on the bottom floor of a building. We were also given another, quite smallish room upstairs where we could store our belongings including the six kilogram slab of bacon we had brought from Latvia. The owner immediately sniffed it out and looked at us in a strange way. She was the widow of a priest.

'You arrived like lords in a carriage, and now look at you, nice and rich with loads of food!' she said.

She couldn't stand us, especially Aivars.

'A boy, dressed in girl's clothes!'

They were Ina's, except for the pants: on his head he wore Ina's warm, little cap, her warm coat and her shoes. Aivars looked like a pretty little girl, blond, blue-eyed with black eyelashes. The "holy" widow appraised Aivars' thin "wooden" legs.

'That boy will never run again,' she said.

My mother gave her a piece of bacon and she immediately changed her attitude, especially toward me.

The ground became covered with a thick layer of snow. I borrowed a children's sleigh from my neighbor and pulled Aivars to the doctor's surgery. The x-rays showed that all of his backbone discs had healed but the doctor said that we should visit him regularly so that I could learn how to massage Aivars' leg muscles properly.

Teddy and I went to the movies. There was an air raid! Everybody shot out of the theater to the air raid shelters but we ran as fast as our legs would carry us on the cobblestone streets towards our apartment. Just the two of us. With the help of the moonlight we found our way in a town that had suddenly become silent. We didn't know if we would reach our children before the bombs began to drop.

Bad news arrived from the battlefield for the Germans. But they countered by claiming the foreign radio broadcasts were lies! But we were listening – we had to run again! Teddy traded his coat for two little coal carts and we started to pack. It was February already, early spring and the sun was warm and the snow had melted. In the night we heard not far away a droning sound; apparently there was a thorough bombardment going on somewhere not far from us. In the morning we were amazed, it was eight a.m. and still dark! We glanced through the window – the whole courtyard was covered with scraps of burnt paper and ash. I ran out and picked up a page – it was a passage from the Bible! I looked back at our house, it was covered with black soot.

We went to the railway station but found there was no room left on the train. We pushed our way with both carts into the baggage wagon and slammed the door shut. The train was going to Dresden. At the first stop the door was yanked open.
  'How did you get in here?'
We were thrown out. We decided to continue our journey by foot in the direction of Bavaria because we thought it would be warmer there. We decided we would only travel along the smaller country roads to try and avoid the bombing. We had to say goodbye to my mother because she

was too old and frail to walk very far. We decided she would take the train to Northern Germany which was already occupied by the British forces. My father, Skaidrīte and little Jānis were said to be there.

My beloved mother, I wondered if I would ever see her again? It tore me apart that she could not come with us. I knew that she was strong and in all ways very enterprising, but to have to leave her all alone! We helped push her into the overcrowded train with her heavy bag strapped to her back (she wasn't about to discard her belongings!) As she climbed the steps onto the train her bag pulled her back onto the platform and my poor mother fell into our arms. The men in the train then woke up and helped to pull her inside.

'Goodbye Mother – we will see you again!'

How close the villages were to one another. You hardly left one before you entered another. The children had lots to see. They sat quietly and were as happy as could be to be able to ride in one of the carts. We walked fast, our feet were not tired yet. A strange, warm wind blew in our faces and blackened tree leaves flew all around us. We saw ahead of us a woman pushing a pram and her husband next to her with a sack on his back and a bag in each hand. Both their faces were blackened, as if from smoke, as was the pram and the blanket covering it.

'Where are you from? What's happened to you?' we asked.

'What do you mean? Don't you know that Dresden was destroyed by the bombing last night[16]?'

They told us that the bombers had dropped phosphorous bombs, people's feet were burned just from running on the pavement. Fleeing from the heat, people ran to the park and jumped into the pond but even the water there was burning and everybody was burned alive. We thought in horror of Elvīra, my brother Vitauts' wife's sister and her two little

---

16   During February 13th - 15th, 1945 Dresden, the baroque capital of the state of Saxony, was bombed in a series of raids by hundreds of British and American bombers. A firestorm destroyed the city center. Today a plaque has been erected stating that almost 100,000 people were killed, many of whom were refugees fleeing from the Soviet advance. The war formerly ended on May 8, 1945.

children and of the many other Latvian refugees. Had they perished in the "safe haven" they had found?

We continued on our way and looked around – there were factories all around us! We increased our stride, sometimes running. The children thought this was great fun! Wherever we looked we couldn't see any air raid shelters. Sure enough, far in the distance we heard the all too familiar sound of the bombers approaching. We threw ourselves into a ditch with both our carts, but the bombers flew over us and we watched as they disappeared over the horizon. It was dusk when we arrived in the next little town. We found a place in the refugee center and lay down on the floor to sleep. And, again an air raid siren sounded! Just as I had closed my eyes! One tall woman shouted that we must run to the shelter. Teddy dressed Aivars, grabbed our documents, and with Aivars under his arm ran off, yelling at me to hurry up. And I did pretend all this time to be hurrying. The same woman returned to scream that the law didn't allow anybody to remain in the building during an air raid. I pretended that I was dressing Atis, who was fast asleep, and the woman hurried off. Together with my baby daughter and youngest son I fell into a deep, deep sleep.

We were on the road again the next day. We got up at six in the morning and got ready to bed down at ten that night. The Germans had appropriated our Soviet passports, but we still had our Latvian passports, which we had hidden. It was a good thing that we had some Latvian five-lat coins with us. They were made of solid silver. I was stingy with them, Teddy was more generous, for which I scolded him. We could buy food with them. On the other hand, when the towns became fewer and we were lucky to find a place to stay at night, I always helped the mistress of the house wash the dishes and in exchange she allowed us to eat some soup and gave us milk, which I warmed up for the children, and let us sleep on the floor. When we left I always cleaned the rooms, if we had slept in the kitchen, I washed the floor.

The farther we walked, the less I ate. I was afraid the Russians would catch up with us or that my children would become ill. Teddy on the other hand always ate up his share, bread with jam, and the children got the best of what we had.

The weather turned cold. It was getting dark one night when we finally reached a small village. We knocked on the first door. The proprietress let us put our children on the floor and warmed them some milk. Teddy went off to look for lodgings for the night. The proprietress was kind. The children sat quietly watching what the adults were doing. It was pitch black when Teddy returned, grabbed the children and put our belongings in the carts.

'Let's go!' he said.

If he behaved in such a hurried manner I knew that he was angry and didn't say a word. I didn't even ask what was wrong. We stopped in front of a big building where an important-looking Nazi official emerged and my husband called to him.

'Put us all in your jail because we don't have a place to spend the night!'

It had begun to snow and the official started making excuses, saying children couldn't be put in jail. He gave us a big wagon with high sides and ordered a Polish prisoner to harness a horse and take us up the hill, but no further. Teddy took off his cap and bowed.

'How generous is the good sir. What a good heart you have, you are going to let my children spend the night in the forest. I thank you!'

I got angry and scolded him.

'Stop, for heaven's sake. When we get to the top of the hill, we'll think of something!'

We loaded Aija and one of the carts into the wagon and sat the boys on top of our other belongings. Teddy followed behind us, pulling the empty cart. I was wearing my skiing outfit, made of thick cotton, a jumper and long pants. The icy wind blew right through me. My little girl, Aija was snug, warmly wrapped up in my fur coat. The boys were covered by blankets. Teddy was wearing his canvas overalls. I feared both of us might get sick. Thankfully, he was a healthy, strong man. I had lost quite a lot of weight and Teddy couldn't stop worrying how I was able to cope with everything and do what had to be done. We climbed the crest of the hill and in the distance spied the lights of a town. The Pole stopped the horse and said that he now had to drive back, but Teddy put his hand in his pocket and barked an order.

'Take us to the town or I will shoot you!'
It was all the same to the Pole so he cracked the whip and commanded the horse to get along.

It was almost midnight by the time we arrived at a refugee care center. The German girls from the center rushed out to receive us.

'We must be getting important guests if they are arriving in a horse-drawn cart!'
They helped us take the children and our belongings into a big room where there was straw on the floor and where other refugees had already quartered themselves. We even got a meal. During this time Teddy found the office to complain about the previous town's snobbish official. The office personnel promised to telephone him the next day and reprimand him. They took my husband for a German. It seemed to me that the straw was not clean and I didn't have any bed sheets so I covered the place where the children would sleep with an expensive table cloth. I had grabbed it as a keepsake, as it was a wedding gift from my mother and my mother-in-law, Veronika Lejiṇa. Having eaten and been washed, my three little children quickly fell asleep. As yet I had never seen them crying or quarreling.

Teddy confessed to me that he had really told off the Nazi official. He shouted at him that the Latvian Legionnaires had earned buckets of medals from the German army for their valiant fighting on the Eastern front but a wise guy in a German town wanted to put him in jail simply because they were missing their German passports. The next morning we hurried away very early – just in case!

Luckily we were able to travel the distance from Freiburg to Chemnitz by train. That way we saved more than a week's traveling time. But as soon as we stepped down from the train – an air raid siren sounded! In the shelter Aija began crying and there was nothing I could do to quieten her. I tried giving her some cold milk to drink. I forgot I had a tin can and a candle in my handbag which I could have used to warm the milk! I tried to console myself that perhaps I would not have been allowed to burn a candle in the air raid shelter.

When we returned to the train we found the cart we used as a pram but the other cart, which had all our belongings stashed in it was gone. We got ready to stay overnight at a refugee center. I was worried. This city was important, it had factories. Why were we taking such a risk? Early in the morning we headed off again, but Teddy went back to the railway station to see if the other cart really was gone. As he was leaving the station building he took a peek behind a door – and there it was! Overjoyed we started to walk to Burgstedt which was not far away. There we found a little room to stay in on the top floor of a house. Aija's temperature began to rise but luckily we were given medicine by a Latvian nurse to cure her lung inflammation. After four days Aija recovered.

An alarm sounded, followed by an announcement – *Da kommen die amerikanen*! (The Americans are coming!) The anxiety we felt was overwhelming. The inhabitants of the house and my family ran down to the cellar. I kept watch, in front of a small window.

'Can you see them?' everybody kept asking me non-stop.

'Oh yes!'

On the top of the hill the first jeeps appeared and sitting in the very first jeep there were four American soldiers! Soon they were pouring down the hill like a river, right towards us. Shots began to crackle and bullets went whizzing by.

'Get away from the window!' Teddy suddenly shouted.

He was very alarmed though in reality we were also overjoyed – now we would be safe! The Germans from the house on the other hand were scared, but not overly scared, because they had heard from German refugee women about the horrors committed by the Russian soldiers.

Even old women were not spared. The younger ones never left their houses, but the Russians forced their way in anyway.

In the evening the landlady told us to return to the cellar because "their boys" were going to attempt to push the Americans back. Nothing doing! We stayed in our warm beds. The next morning the landlady told us that there had been a battle in Burgstedt.

'Weren't you afraid?' she asked.

We had to admit that we had heard nothing. She was astounded because right there, not far from the house, one building had been totally destroyed. The German soldiers had decided to make their last stand there. We must have slept the sleep of the dead!

A few days later Teddy was gazing through the window of our room wondering if he would see any Americans?

'Yes, there's two of them strolling past right now!' Teddy said excitedly.

Teddy invited them in English to come up to our room, he had a bottle of wine, and wanted to welcome them. I also came to the window with my little girl in my arms.

'Okay!' They said.

We ran downstairs and opened the door. Atis and Aivars stared, wide-eyed at the soldiers, especially Aivars, because he could see that the American soldiers looked different from the German soldiers.

We told them our story and soon the bottle was empty. The soldiers were happy that we were not German so they knew they had nothing to fear from us. They were very surprised to learn that the Russians were our enemies, they thought they were America's friend. It was news to them that the Communists could be so cruel. I began to fret about this and didn't hear one of them ask the other one, who was Jewish, what time they had to be back at their unit. I interrupted and inquired when the Russians would be arriving in Burgstedt. The Jewish soldier looked at his watch.

'At three o'clock,' he said.

I collapsed but Teddy caught me and lifted me back onto my feet.

'What's the matter?' the soldiers asked.

We explained.

'Well, if you are so afraid of the Russians then you should move away as quickly as possible,' one of them said.

Exactly when the Russians would arrive, they couldn't say but they did say they could come during the night. They bid us farewell and one of them even patted Atis and Aivars on the head.

The next morning we were off again. In the afternoon we heard artillery fire. Suddenly an American sentry appeared and ordered us to stop! He told us we were not allowed to go on this road. It was a firing zone. We had to turn back.

What now! We stayed put. Two other soldiers, quite young, came up to us, one of whom appeared to be angry. They took Teddy away with them for questioning. The sentry began to munch on a chocolate bar. Then looked at us. His face was a bit dark, maybe he was Mexican? He called Aivars and Atis over to him and gave them a chocolate bar each. The boys were all smiles. Atis offered his to Aija but she refused to eat it.

We spent about two hours sitting on the roadside by a ditch. My heart was giving out. Finally Teddy was led back by two new sentries. We were told we had to go back along the same road we had come from. We retreated a bit of the way and found ourselves in a small village. Further back the road did not lead anywhere. We made a detour over the potato fields, struggling over the bumps of the newly ploughed furrows. The carts periodically fell over and everything spilled out, including the children. We quickly put the children and everything back in again and continued to struggle through the mud. In the end we got out of the field and onto a narrow, unpaved road. I saw small houses and next to them, on the right, a big tree and some bushes. I went towards them to reconnoiter the area. Three American soldiers crawled out of the bushes and ordered me to go back.

'This is a firing zone!' they shouted.

But I launched into a discussion with them. I told them we had come so far with our small children and we needed to keep going. (Teddy had hidden himself behind the cart with our belongings.)

'No!' they said. 'No, you can't go this way!'

I began to sing.

'Oh, darkies how my heart grows weary, far, far away from home…'
They at once joined me, and I continued to stay put. Suddenly one of them, probably a sergeant, turned to the others.

'She is a pretty girl. I'll take her through the town,' he announced.

'Thank you, thank you…' I said, clapping my hands.
As if I had wings I flew back to my family. When the sergeant saw Teddy he was surprised but didn't say anything. Teddy later told me that this same sergeant was the one who had previously arrested him and wouldn't allow him to speak to the commander until he had convinced him that not everybody who spoke German and English was a spy, furthermore not someone with a wife and three kids in tow. In the end he allowed Teddy to speak to the commander and was freed.

The sergeant strode rapidly and my face became soaked in sweat. He said that he would have helped me to pull the pram-cart but he couldn't do it with a rifle in his hand.

'Why don't you wear make-up?' he asked.

'My goodness! Makeup! I'm tired and scared to death and you are talking about make-up!'
He went on to tell me his wife applied cosmetics to her face no matter how tired she was, this was a "must" for her.

'How old are you?'

'40.'

'I don't believe you. Pretty girls deliberately add on some years just to hear how young they look.'

'Thank you!'
In this way, chatting and laughing, we passed through the town. Before he departed he wrote a chit to the commander in the next village to give us a night's lodgings for free and biscuits for the children. Atis and

Aivars were beside themselves with joy over the Americans - we had finally reached the Americans zone.

Aija ate very little, just like me. I had lost so much weight it seemed that my bones had begun to rattle. We were running from early in the morning until late at night… I could hardly feel my legs anymore. Around midnight my head would start to spin, I'd reel as I washed the children and then I'd fall into a deep slumber. The next morning we had to move faster, the Russians were just behind us! Teddy started to throw things out of his cart. When he was not looking (having a smoke) I retrieved some of them and hid them in my "pram". I regretted salvaging the iron though because we could not use it in that country!

We began using country lanes to avoid being seen. Late in the evening we found a house with a kind landlady. The children were put in a spare room and Teddy and I even got a bed to sleep in. In the morning I put everything back in order and helped the landlady do the dishes and told her about us. It was a very friendly departure, she pressed a lump of bacon into my hand for the journey.

We walked a very long way and reached Salfeldt. Here we were told that the whole province of Thüringen was going to be handed over to the Russians. Our nerves were once again pulled as tight as wire. The German refugees were streaming to the south, Russian prisoners to the north. Suddenly a truck full of Russian political commissars, with red ribbons around their caps, drove past us. I staggered, and clutched my heart, it had almost stopped beating. We had to move on faster and faster, and faster. To Coburg!

We stopped to have a snack at the foot of a hill. My watch showed eleven in the morning. I wondered if we would reach the next village by nightfall? A German woman came down the hill and Teddy asked her how long it would take to get to the top?

'*Zwei stunden laufen,*' (Two hours if you hurry) she said.

I was still pulling my cart after midday, trailed by Teddy who was pulling the cart filled with our belongings. What beautiful fir trees there were all around us! The children were tied to the "pram" and gazed in wonder at the huge trees. We dragged ourselves in a zigzag pattern up the steep slope. Teddy had a heavy load and every now and then I climbed down to help him push his cart up to where the children were. On and on we went. Five hours had passed and we stopped for another snack but I couldn't eat the bread and marmalade. I had lost my appetite. The children drank milk, Teddy and I, water.

It had taken us eight hours! Dusk was setting in and we could hardly drag ourselves any further. The children had become silent, only occasionally one of them would whisper something to the other. What a fearful silence! Suddenly I felt like my insides had started to climb up inside me.

'Oh, if only the Pearly Gates would appear and open to receive us!' I exclaimed in desperation.

And, truly, I saw them open, and we were sitting in the dining hall of a castle at a long table, covered with a white table cloth. At the table all three of my beloved ones sat opposite Teddy and I with such clean, rosy cheeks as I had never ever seen before. From the ceiling a crystal chandelier was spreading radiant light. I sank into a soft, white bed. Oh, it was ever so soft! I looked at the ceiling, it was blue, as were the walls. Where was I? What was this? I was lying on a cloud, my hand disappeared into it. I feared I would fall down to the ground. I came back with a start! I was still pulling my cart.

'Can't you hear the children crying? Why are you running through the village! Come back!' I heard Teddy shouting from far behind me.

It was dark. Here and there somebody opened a door only to slam it shut again. What was happening to me? Was I losing my mind? I heard Teddy yelling at me to quieten the children.

'No!' I retorted, 'Let them cry even louder, perhaps somebody with a heart will hear.'
A woman ran up to us and invited us to spend the night in her cottage. It was already midnight.

The woman's husband had either fallen in battle or been taken prisoner. She put her two little boys in the attic, in a built-in niche. Our children were put in beds. I dropped down on the kitchen floor in front of the stove. I can't remember where Teddy slept, probably with the children. The landlady told us the Russians would also be coming there as well. Nevertheless we stayed one more night. I think I gave her the last of my silk stockings from Latvia and the boy's two new, white caps. We still had some "mildas", the big heavy five lat silver Latvian coins, hidden for emergencies.

We left there and after another day's travel, in the distance we spied the buildings of a big farm. I entered the courtyard. In the barn there were many cows. The lady of the farm and her maids were tending to them. The farmer came up to us and Teddy explained who we were and asked for a night's lodgings. We were led up to the top floor. The house was not exactly a castle, but near enough. The long corridor and many rooms on either side each told a story. Life must have been quite grand there once. Our wing appeared to be empty. The room we were shown to had a wooden floor with four beds and a table. The maid turned down the beds and brought us warm, tasty food on a tray three times a day. The next day it started to rain and it rained non-stop for a whole week. We were lucky that we didn't have to leave. The children could run about and play from morning till evening. Nobody disturbed us. Teddy and I lived the life of a count and countess.

Finally it stopped raining. The lord of the manor offered to take us part of the way up the hill. We wondered in amazement why he was so forthcoming. Perhaps he was afraid of the Americans. Maybe his family had some ties with the Nazis? Bidding us farewell he said that Coburg was not far away and, laughing, told us that we slept in the same room where Napoleon once stayed the night! What luck that we didn't have to drag ourselves up that steep hill!

We reached Bavaria. The Bavarians would not allow us to stay overnight in their homes. At one house Teddy didn't give up so easily as there was a sign above the door, *Sei villkommen in diesem Hause* (Welcome To This House). As we left he turned the sign around. Then, as had often happened before, a poorer household received us in their dimly lit home. After a while there was a knock on the door – a policeman entered. We were supposed to have *demoliert* (vandalized) a house. My husband explained what happened and the officer left, telling us not to do such things in the future.

One beautiful day around midday, we were walking along a highway as heavy American trucks roared past us. We had begun looking earlier for places where we could spend the night, closer to the highway. We asked a village "elder" where we could stay overnight. This gentleman, a miller, pointed to a shed by the roadside. I ran over to take a look. Horror! The wooden floor was absolutely filthy. The Russian prisoners who had been quartered there, possibly in revenge against the Germans, had defecated all over it! I called my husband over to see this "boudoir". The miller remained standing, watching us. Clearly he was thinking something about us. He knew Teddy spoke German well and that I was a foreigner. As always Teddy was outraged and accosted the miller.

'You want my wife to die cleaning this place, and our little children… I will complain to the Americans, because I can speak English.'

At that moment an American truck sped past. We decided that Teddy would pretend to flag down a truck but at that very moment I would call him and ask him to quickly return to me. Hopefully, these maneuvers would leave the impression on the miller that Teddy let the truck pass unintentionally. As another heavy truck appeared, I ran up to Teddy, scolding him, and in the commotion he "missed" his chance to stop the truck. We had to wait a longer time for the next truck but before it arrived the miller's nerves gave way and he offered us his house.

We beamed. The children were as silent as mice, observing everything with intense curiosity – something was happening again! Usually people praised us about how quiet our children were. Aija was already in her tenth month and the war had just ended. She wanted to run like her brothers but still couldn't. Atis was always helping his little sister, but Aivars ignored her. He was happy now that he could run himself.

The building was unusual, it was joined onto the mill. They were rich people, everything was big, in the German style. We were shown to a place in one of the family rooms. The conversation was friendly, the food excellent. We even ate apples – and got some to take along for the journey the next day. We departed on friendly terms, but to get milk we had to "fight" a bit. The miller's wife fed the milk into a centrifuge which separated the cream from the milk. She poured skimmed milk for my children but I asked for her permission to give them full cream milk.

'Skimmed milk is just as good,' she said.

'But my children have never drunk anything but full cream milk.'

In the end they got to drink delicious, warm, "real" milk.

In Coburg, an American sentry stopped us at a post. He lit a cigarette and offered one to Teddy, who was elated that we had finally reached safety, with the Americans. Their conversation dragged on. I nudged my husband to let him know it was time to get going. Who knew, we could get arrested. He ignored me. A changing of sentries took place and the new soldiers decided to take us to the refugee filtration station where the Russians repatriated refugees back to their homeland. Had we managed to come so far only to…

We were all put into the back of a truck. There was no room for the second cart so we were told to leave it by a tree and pick it up later. Teddy had now turned pale and couldn't utter a word. Two G.I.'s sat next to us, crunching on cookies.

'Are they tasty?' I asked.

One of them passed us a whole bag. I praised them and America. Fortunately on the way to Coburg we had met a Latvian woman who had given us her address in that city. It finally got through to the soldiers that I could speak English.

'She can speak English!' one of the soldiers exclaimed in surprise. I begged them to take us to our "relative" right here in Coburg. The soldiers ordered the driver to take us to the commander to ask for permission to do that. Teddy came out of the headquarters smiling and off we went again, this time in search of the address we had given them. What would we do when we got there?

Teddy had a plan. When we arrived at the destination, he embraced the surprised woman and quickly whispered in her ear.
'Please do as I say. Save us!'
What a wonderful reunion! Our "Aunty" greeted each and every one of us in turn as the soldiers watched on. Teddy even ran up to them and gave them a bottle of vodka which he had kept for emergencies. They grabbed it with glee and joyfully waved to us as the truck roared off quicker than we could wave back.

But the German landlady had no intention whatsoever of allowing refugees to stay in her boarder's room. Teddy ran off to a nearby hotel but there were no rooms available. In the evening he tried again. Nothing. Then we put our children in the "pram" and we all went to the hotel together. We kept it under surveillance and spied somebody moving out of his room. We immediately went and occupied it. We informed the duty clerk who we were and which room we were in and asked if the good clerk would please hand over the keys. It worked! We were safe!

The next day Teddy rushed over to the tree where we had left the second cart. Exactly at the moment when he arrived a man was just starting to drag it away. Teddy's severe countenance however convinced the stranger to give the cart back without offering any resistance.

The money which Teddy saved working at the Sebnitz warehouse had run out. All we had left were five Reichmarks which a passer-by had given us. It happened like this: we were dragging our carts, panting and sweating. A man came up to my husband and inquired if it was hard to pull the carts?

'By no means,' Teddy replied. 'We're just playing horses.'

Then the fellow opened up his wallet, took out five marks, and gave them to Teddy.

'Danke schoen!' (Thank you very much!)

I washed the little ones in a basin and put them to bed. I was the last one to go to bed. I observed myself standing naked in front of the half mirror. Oh my! After four months of "traveling" from Sebnitz my breasts had become like two pancakes hanging over my ribs… but my face didn't look too bad, suntanned and healthy. Teddy on the other hand had not lost any weight, he looked brown as an Arab! Aija and Atis were rather thin but Aivars, well, he looked alright.

I began to review our food storage. We had loads of peas and beans stashed away in small bags - why hadn't I thrown them out! There was more than enough of them available here. And there was my mother's lump of bacon, it had turned yellow having melted under the hot sun while in the cart, and had left a stripe on the road as a sign that we had traveled there!

We found out that there was a Latvian club in Coburg. A new life began for us there. My husband and I began to teach English at the club. During that time Aivars was charged with looking after Atis, to play with him in the park. Aija was left in our room but tied to one leg of the bed so that she could crawl all over the room. I left the door open so that if she started to cry the neighbors would come – they looked honest enough. We were only gone for two hours. I opened the door and saw little Aija fast asleep on the floor. I hurried off to the park.

'Where's Atis?' I asked Aivars.

'He was here just now.'

Atis was nowhere in the park!

'Have you seen a small boy with funny footwear that looks like duck's feet?' I asked an old man sitting on a bench.

'Indeed yes. He ran off along the street in that direction,' he said pointing.

'Atis! Atis!' I called as I ran along the street.

Ahead of me I saw American soldiers standing by a church. I ran up to them.

'Have you seen a small, dark-haired boy?'

'Oh, you mean the one with those funny slippers!'

There he was sitting up on a wall nearby with his mouth full of chocolate and his face covered in chocolate. Another group of soldiers was laughing and showing him tricks. Crying, I grabbed him, pressed him to my breast and gave him a good whack on his bottom. But the soldiers came to his defense.

When I settled down I began a conversation with them, telling them about our journey and why we had fled to the Americans for help. They were astounded.

'But the Russians are our friends!'

'Remember my words. The Russians will also rob you of your freedom if they become stronger than you!'

We were all happily reunited back in our room. But what had happened? All our bags had been opened and pieces of our clothing stolen! The next day we took the children with us to the club, then after that we organized ourselves in the following manner; my husband went first. When he returned, I went.

Rumors abounded that the Americans were going to send us back to Latvia. Teddy walked the streets wondering what we should do? To start pulling and dragging the carts again, this time to northern Germany, to the British zone of occupation, seemed like too much of a struggle. His brother, Jānis was living in London; there was hope that we could get travel visas to Great Britain. In 1905, when Jānis was only fourteen he began his seaman's career and never returned home. He settled in London, where Teddy saw him again in 1920 when he was working at the Latvian consulate. It was June, if we walked it would take us until December to reach Northern Germany. We couldn't hitchhike in trucks, who would take us with children?

Then one day Teddy saw a German soldier still in his "uniform" standing next to a horse the size of a large dog and in place of a cart, a big box with two rubber wheels. He went up to him and said how lucky he was – to have a horse and cart!

'No. On the contrary,' the German replied.
He was as unhappy as could be.

'Clothe me, give me some tobacco and a bicycle and then you can have the horse and cart.'

'Just you wait here awhile, you will get everything!' Teddy promised.

Teddy dashed back to the hotel. Luckily he had saved a big wad of tobacco and taken two of his best suits with him from Latvia. The most expensive of these, tailor made from the best wool in the Latvian Army's Economics Department Store, would go to the soldier. But where would we get a bicycle from? Just then the door opened and a Latvian asked my husband to translate some papers into English. He was getting ready to flee to the French zone.

'Do you by any chance have a bicycle?' Teddy asked.
'Of course. Two even!'

We decided there and then that both families would travel together to the British zone. Our compatriot also had a wife and two children.

So we began to trek again, over fields, the further away from Coburg the better. The children and our belongings were in the cart, the adults on foot beside it. We arrived at a village where the man in charge assigned an empty room to us as our temporary shelter. Our traveling companions were given the room next door. I requested some food from the Germans but was refused. I raised a din. The man in charge arrived.

'We are not Russians. Latvia doesn't belong to Russia and we have our consul in London!' I told him.

'Well now, *Gnaedige Frau*, (my most esteemed lady) you even have a consul in London!'

Still, he ordered food for us and the most important thing of all – milk for the children.

Alarm! The Americans were said to be sending back refugees to Latvia! After all, we were refugees who longed to return to our homeland! My husband ran off to the man in charge and told him that we had been friends with the Germans, and that he had donated his expensive coat to the Latvian Legion, et cetera. The "head" replied that he had not received any orders to detain refugees, but he could well get them tomorrow. He advised us to disappear immediately. My traveling lady friend had just washed her family's linen and protested that we had to wait until it was dry. My husband made short shrift of that.

'Pack everything into the cart - now!'

Although our companion grumbled we were ready in a jiffy and off we went.

But what would we do without documents at the American zone's border? We had none, nor did they. But the man, who had been a barman in his younger years, had a good idea. Teddy should ride his bicycle, dressed in his English overalls, carrying six year old Aivars in front, in the basket – no papers were demanded from such travelers. The rest of us should then follow and I ought to be able to talk our way past the guards.

At the zone's border there was a long line. We observed that no-one stopped Teddy and Aivars. We were nervous. Our turn came.

'Permit please!'

'What permit? Didn't my husband show it to you? The one in the English overalls!'

'What English overalls?' two American soldiers replied. 'What are you talking about?'

They started to laugh. I tried to smile. After all this was so ridiculous. I started to sing.

'It's a long way to Tipperary...' – and the soldiers immediately joined in.

Everybody waited nervously, but we continued to talk nonsense without end. Finally one of the G.I.'s turned to the other.

'She speaks English – let her pass.'

Then he bowed to me and wished me good luck.

But we still had to get to the British zone. We decided to head in the direction of the sea, closer to England, just in case we needed to run again. We thought if we had to we could hop onto a boat and paddle off to England! We searched for a place to stay overnight. If we saw the farmer's wife on a farm, Teddy approached her first and brought her around with his good German. Up until then he had always managed. This time he returned, sighing.

'The proprietress is getting on in years and refused to bend.'

She said she would let us stay in the shed instead. Our friends were willing to accept this, but not us. I could also be obstinate. I took Aija by the hand, found the lady, and pleaded with her to let us sleep on the floor in her house.

'My children are very quiet.'

'But maybe you have lice?'

I pretended that I didn't quite hear her.

'What! You have lice!' I cried out. 'In that case we will not sleep here. I'm a teacher and I'm used to cleanliness.'

She hurried to explain that that was not what she had meant... but I interrupted her.

'Oh how wonderful that you don't have lice and that everything is clean. *Danke schoen, vielen Dank!'* (Thank you, thank you very much!) I embraced her. Confused, she showed us to a clean room which had soft carpets from wall to wall. She even treated us to manna porridge with dumplings in milk.

The next day we still came across many Americans. A jolly German fellow gave us a place to stay, in a room of his tavern, where long tables and chairs were stored. We pushed the tables together and slept on them. But soon enough in the next room the noise got louder. A party was going on with American soldiers and German girls, and the decibel level soon rose to the uppermost limits. The action was also taking place outside, on the staircase, where one of the girls was struggling with an apparently very eager young fellow. Teddy got angry. He got up, knocked on the door and said that his wife and kids couldn't sleep. I opened the door that led to the staircase, and saw that the eager soldier was endeavoring to "make out" with his girl in the small space under the stairs. I quickly slammed the door. For a while there was quiet but then everything began all over again. The boys and girls who had paired off walked from the guest room through our room, in order to get to the staircase. My husband always slept soundly. As soon as he put his head down on the folded blankets he dropped off to sleep. I was also getting used to the noise in the guest room but this business in the staircase and constant opening and closing of the door deprived me of sleep. Then the boys and girls endeavored to tiptoe past us but after that I only snatched a little sleep.

We were up at six the next morning. One sleepy American entered from the guest room, sat down by one of the tables and apologized for the antics of the previous night. He showed us a picture of his bride and said he was worried that she might not be waiting for him when he got home. He was enthralled by our children, and performed all kinds of tricks for them before he retired. The owner of the tavern also came and apologized but one had to make allowances for the boys, he said.

'They are so far away from their country.'
Soon we were on the road again.

Further north there were no more villages. The farms were spaced well apart from each other, like they were in Latvia. It was nice walking on the road where we met only the odd traveler. Alongside the road apple trees grew and the fruit was ripe. Our traveling companions felt no compunction about shaking down the trees and picking up the apples. Every now and then we reminded them that some apples should be left for the owners of the trees too! In the fields there were potatoes and carrots galore, also there our companions "gathered in the harvest". I told Teddy to also go and fetch a few carrots for our vitamin share! I had never seen such a frightened "thief" as my husband. I couldn't stop myself from laughing… He crept out into the field, quickly yanked out a few carrots, then looked furtively in all directions in case he had been seen by the owner! The other couple just waded into the field and picked a whole basket. They said they would also provide us with lunch. We would not have to do anything. The former barman had a fantastic ability to make a meal meant for nine into a meal for eighteen! Butter, eggs, milk, as much as you please – for five children and four adults!

But then our little black horse developed a sore on his neck from the harness. Everybody gave my husband advice on what to do to alleviate the poor creature's pain. Animals and birds had always been dear to my husband, he had been a farmer himself once.

'If only we had a soft, rabbit skin…' my lady friend observed.

'Well, give me the rabbit skin,' my husband retorted.

Somehow we dealt with it, probably by rubbing the harness with butter which we also used to "grease" the axels to make the wheels turn more easily.

After this nothing really too dramatic happened, except that Aivars fell out of the front of the cart straight under the horse's legs but the horse halted immediately.

We walked through the town of Kassel and a frightening silence descended upon us. The streets were desolate, on either side there was nothing but ruins, with chimney stacks rising mournfully into the sky. Here and there wreaths lay on top of the ruins. It seemed like we walked for a long time. Even the children talked to each other only in whispers.

We all felt the "fire of hell" that had eaten alive the people who had perished all around and, oh the children…

We moved on to the next town and spent the night in a building on the second floor. There was nobody else on that floor. Having heard that Latvians were gathering together in this town and that they were being given temporary permits, Teddy jumped on his bike and pedaled off to where this was being done. On the way he became hot and drank a whole jug of cold beer and then headed back home after registering us at the permit center. A strong wind arose and the bicycle's steering mechanism broke down. Screaming for people to get out of the way, he flew down the hill.

'I'm freezing to death!' he called out to me in the night.

He was unable to stop shaking and was shivering all over. I wrapped him up in all the blankets we had but it didn't help. I ran down to the kitchen and boiled water, filling up every available bottle. The landlady ran up and down the stairs helping me in every way possible. The hot bottles warmed him up. He broke out into a sweat. A new day dawned. After a few more days we were on our way again.

We reached the town of Oldenburg in September, 1945. Together with other refugees we were quartered in the "Fine Arts House" – and once again found ourselves on the top floor. We were told that after a few weeks we would be moved to Ohmstede, a Latvian refugee camp, which was next to Oldenburg. Teddy however had started to cough quite badly. His brown face had a green tinge to it. He didn't look good. He couldn't carry up our heavy wooden suitcase. Two weeks later he was still coughing. I ran up and down to the kitchen and back, continuously washing the dishes and did not allow the children near him in case he was contagious. Everything that I had saved along the way from the German farmers; eggs, honey, apples and the butter we had bought with our "mildas", I fed into him until the food started to trickle out his ears. By the time we had to move to the camp he was healed.

We lived in Ohmstede and then in another camp in Fallingbostel until 1950. We tried to immigrate to America but Teddy was rejected because a TB hole was found in one of his lungs. Later, when we went through health-checks to immigrate to Australia Teddy was again rejected because of the TB hole. The Australian doctor said he only had three more months to live! It took a long time and many x-rays before we could prove the opposite – that the hole had calcified and the man was fit and healthy! In the end we got the green light.

We were finally taken by the International Refugee Organization on the American troop carrier ship the *General Black* to Australia.

But that is a very different story indeed – the worst part was over.

Ohmstede, refugee camp in Germany 1948.
Aija in front, Aivars behind her and Atis next to father on right

Chapter 7

Reclaiming the past: a son returns home to fight for Latvia's future

Atis Lejiņš

We arrived in Australia in 1950 and settled down in the suburb of Greensborough on the outskirts of Melbourne in a house built by one of the first settlers over a hundred years before. The little gravel road leading to it was named after him – Poulter Avenue. The house was made of big, square rocks, dried mud and straw and it only had two rooms. The walls were very thick and it was cool inside during summer. An additional three rooms made up the wooden extension that had been built onto the original stone structure. One of them was the kitchen where most of our indoor activities took place since this was where the stove was and the big kerosene fed lamp. You pumped it and it radiated a very bright light over the whole room. The house had no electricity and we hardly had to pay anything for rent to the landlord who had a farm not very far away. We also had a farm of sorts – forty hens, three cows and a large vegetable garden. We all ate well, and I used to lug cucumbers up the hill and sell them to the local grocery shop.

We were living simply in order to save enough money to move to America. Dad's cousin, Hamilkars and his wife Zenta, who fled to Sweden during the war and later moved to California, had invited us to come. My dad was afraid the Chinese communists could come "down under" and take over Australia. So the strategic plan was for us to emigrate to America and once and for all be safe.

When I was fourteen I ran into the kitchen one hot summer's day and found my mother crying.

'What's happened?' I asked.

She told me that my grandfather, Kristaps Irbe had died in Germany. My grandmother, Paulīne Jostsone-Irbe had died a few years earlier. I only had the faintest recollection of my grandparents because they had lived in a different refugee camp and we only visited them once I think. My grandmother had been reunited with her husband and her daughter, Skaidrīte in northern Germany after the war. My grandfather and my Aunty Skaidrīte had fled from Uncle Kocis' parents' farm straight to the British zone of occupation in Germany. Skadrīte heard that her husband Kocis had fallen while fighting on the Eastern front.

Our Latvian friends from inner Melbourne often visited us. For them it was like a trip to the countryside. The Plenty River flowed just a few meters from our house and the men folk caught eels there. There were lots of them because Australians don't eat eels. My job was to kill and pluck a couple of chickens and lug big, brown bottles of beer back home from the pub down the hill for our guests.

Once when we were all seated at one such gathering I felt an unusual silence in the room. I heard talk of the war in French Indochina. The elders spoke in subdued tones about Latvian soldiers dying there. They had joined the French Foreign Legion after the war because they were afraid they would be handed over to the Russians. Two of our guests were former Latvian soldiers who had been mobilized by the Germans and fought in the so-called Latvian Legion. I heard that the French outpost called *Dien Bien Phu*, which had been besieged for months, had finally fallen to the Vietnamese guerrilla leader, Ho Chi Min. I also heard the two former soldiers say that many Latvian soldiers perished there, together with thousands of soldiers from other nationalities, but most were German, serving in the French Foreign Legion.

Every summer I travelled to the fruit growing district of Paringa, named after the Aboriginal word meaning "big bend in the river" in northern, South Australia, near the town of Renmark. I went there to help my Uncle Vincis and Aunty Skaidrīte on their 40 acre fruit block by the Murray River. Aunty Skaidrīte had met and married Uncle Vincis in a refugee camp in Germany. I picked apricots all day in the baking hot sun with my cousin, Jānis and his little brother, Vidvuds who was born in Australia. When all the boxes were full we loaded them onto a trailer. Then Uncle Vincis drove us and the boxes to the shed by the Murray river on the back of his big, red, Massey Ferguson tractor. There we split the apricots in half with a knife which had a curved blade and placed them on boards to dry in the sun. We ate a lot of apricots, they were big, sweet and juicy. We also ate peaches and oranges straight from the trees. We got plenty of vitamins and minerals.

Once I complained that life was hard.

'If you want to know what hard life is all about read, *Dvēseļu putens* (Blizzard of Souls),' Uncle Vincis retorted. 'Then you'll think twice before complaining. We have it easy here.'

He was a former soldier who sang soldier songs without end as he worked beside us. He had joined the Latvian Legion at seventeen years of age in order to escape an arranged marriage that his mother had organized with a woman who was ten years older than him.

When I returned home to Greensborough at the end of summer I did read *Dvēseļu putens*. I was sixteen and it was the first Latvian book I had read. On the very first page the protagonist, a soldier, also sixteen, had joined the Latvian National Liberation Army in 1919 and had just fallen in love with a girl in Rīga. I had also fallen in love for the first time and was taken by the soldier's courage to put his life on the line in such a seemingly hopeless situation. The Latvian army appeared to be no match for the big German and Russian armies. I couldn't put the book down, even though it took me an hour to get through the first page. My mother had taught me basic Latvian but previously I'd had no interest in reading any Latvian books. I'd been busy playing the noble Indian brave, with my bow and arrows, who always managed to outwit the American army, even though my heroes were Hopalong Cassidy and Tom Mix. These cowboy classics were shown to us kids by the British soldiers at their base which was not far from our camp in Falinbostel, Germany. We always got chewing gum then, a great treat!

The day when we were to leave for America was fast approaching. I was seventeen and quite aware of what was going on, unlike when I was seven, when we boarded the American troop carrier ship, the *General Black* in Naples, Italy after a long train journey from Northern Germany. This time I knew there was a past, a present and an unknown future. We had become Australian citizens, subjects of Her Majesty Queen Elizabeth II of England, and at last could afford to buy tickets for the long cruise across the mighty Pacific to Los Angeles, where Uncle Hamilkars and Aunty Zenta were waiting for us.

What would the future bring? I sat in the willow tree next to the kitchen and watched the big, red sun sink below the horizon. Now remember young man, I said to myself over and over again, remember this time when you had no idea what the future would bring. When you are old, come back to this willow and the setting sun and then you will be able to see your future because you will have lived it. But what did the future hold for me?

America decided to step in and continue to fight Ho Chi Min and his guerrillas after the French were beaten and left Vietnam. Washington thought that if the anti-French resistance gained power, Communist China would take over Vietnam, and after that, one Asian country after another. It was called the domino effect.

I sat in the amphibious landing craft clutching my M14 rifle together with the other marines in my company. The gap between our landing craft and the shore was rapidly diminishing. The sick feeling in my stomach grew bigger, but it was not caused by the landing craft bouncing over the waves. While we were still in the troop carrier ship our sergeant had told us that ninety percent of men in the first assault wave get killed or wounded. I was in the first wave.

The bullets coming from the enemy's machine gun nest cut us down, or so it seemed. If they had been real bullets and not plastic ones, would I have been hit and would that have been the end of me? The war exercises for us reservists, held off the coast of Southern California, ended successfully when we took the island. But the real war in Vietnam was gearing up and America was torn by dissent - was this the right war for the right cause?

I returned to the sweltering prairie in Iowa. It was summer and I was living in Des Moines, working with a Latvian friend to earn my way through college. I was enrolled at the University of California in Los Angeles. Our construction crew was made up of three Latvian-Americans. We rushed off to the closest bar a good way from where we were building houses. I held my breath as we watched the big TV screen that would decide whether I would be called up for active service in Vietnam. Lyndon B. Johnson, who had taken over the presidency after John F. Kennedy's assassination, made an announcement.

'I have decided not to call up the reserves...' he said in his Texan drawl. Everybody in the room cheered and I had to shout drinks all round.

I went back to Los Angeles and lived in the run-down suburb of Venice, by the beach, where the rent was cheap and I could run along the edge of the Pacific Ocean and stay in good condition despite all the history and political science books I had to read for my exams. I switched from electrical engineering which I had been studying at Melbourne Senior Technical College to humanities at UCLA. I wanted to know why humans acted the way they did, why I was not living in the country of my birth.

I was awoken by a phone call from my sister, Aija.

'Atis, did you hear, our Sirhan has shot Edward Kennedy!'

We were shocked - how could our friend have taken such a drastic step to further the Palestinian cause by killing a US presidential candidate? While attending Pasadena High School, a satellite city of Los Angeles, my sister and I took German classes with Sirhan who befriended us because he wanted to know what the Soviet Union was like.

He could hardly believe what we said about it but listened attentively and kept asking questions about what happened to Latvia. He never argued with us, never tried to refute our claims. He just listened. It seemed that he carefully weighed every word we said. We in turn knew nothing about Israel or Palestine, and heard him out.

I discovered that for many people the Second World War did not end on May 8, 1945. I learned this from a Latvian writer, Andrievs (Andy) Salmiņš who was some ten years older than me. Every Friday evening we would sit in the *Oar House*, a bar close to the beach in Venice during "Happy Hour" when you got peanuts for free. I bought the pitchers of beer for half-price and Andy talked about politics and history. His hands and part of his face had been disfigured in a road accident in Rīga during the war when the car he and his parents were traveling in ran into a German army truck carrying acid.

He had read all the books I was yet to read, and many more. I suspected he was a genius. He studied sociology and I tried to use his insights to understand how the Soviet Union functioned. He introduced me to the book *The Power Elite*, by C. Wright Mills but the notes I made in the margins related more to the Soviet Union than to America. From Andy I found out that another million people died after the war until finally the "peoples' democracies" were established in central Europe with the help of Soviet tanks. He also disclosed what no book at UCLA said - that guerrilla warfare against the Soviet occupation in the Baltics had only recently been stamped out - in the mid fifties! That was just ten years ago! And that the many brave, young, Latvian men who were sent from Sweden to Latvia after the end of the war to support the guerrillas had all been betrayed by the master British agent for the Soviet Union, Kim Philby, who had access to information about the clandestine operations. The Latvians walked straight into a trap and were left to the tender mercies of the KGB!

In the summer of 1968 I found myself in West Berlin, an outpost of freedom separated from West Germany by communist East Germany.

I was there to read a paper on the Soviet subjugation of Central and Eastern Europe to the First World Latvian Youth Congress. But suddenly the West German government served notice that we were to cancel the congress and move it to Hanover in West Germany if we wanted to hold it. We refused - and created a sensation in Germany. The mass media was soon upon us, and for the first time since the war Latvia's name was heard throughout Germany. We told the microphones and TV cameras of Germany that we believed West Berlin to be a free city and we would go ahead with the congress as planned.

The City of Berlin was divided by a wall running through the middle of it. West Berlin belonged to West Germany, while East Berlin belonged to communist East Germany. The only way to enter West Berlin from West Germany was by plane, though I think you could also travel by car or rail if you had a special permit from the East German authorities. The railway was sealed and you could only exit in West Berlin, so West Berlin was a special case, hence it was full of U.S., British and French troops. In fact, because it was surrounded by East Germany it was indefensible but an attack on West Berlin would have most likely started another world war because it was considered a symbol of freedom to the rest of the world. Between East and West Berlin was the famous *Check Point Charlie*, where both sides often swapped spies. Our case showed that when put to the test the same democratic rules that applied to West Germany proper did not apply to West Berlin. I think we made history on that point.

West Berlin was still formally under occupation by the Western Allies; America, Great Britain and France, as was East Germany by Russia, i.e. the Soviet Union. West Germany turned to the Western Allies for help. What would they say? They decided to back West Germany. An American army jeep with three soldiers and a mounted machine gun arrived at the door of the building where we were ensconced. We went out and spoke with the driver, who was all smiles. But the soldiers' arrival left an impression on the European Latvians. They got telephone calls from their elders saying that if we didn't surrender we would be sent to concentration camps in Alaska. They caved in to the pressure and I, the ring leader of the "resistance", was left in a minority. I realized if we were split, then we had lost. Only in unity is there strength.

'We are defeated. Let's retreat with dignity,' I told my followers.

Before we departed I snuck off to the observation platform by the Wall in West Berlin, which is near the famous Brandenburg Gate on the communist side. Just across from the platform was the Soviet military monument dedicated to the Soviet army divisions that had captured Berlin twenty-three years earlier. There was a Soviet soldier standing there. He gaped in surprise when I shook my fist at him! Who knows, maybe he was a hapless Latvian inducted into the Soviet army?

We American Latvians didn't give up so easily. We held the congress in Hanover and afterwards some two hundred of us, in three hired buses, barreled down the autobahn to the American embassy in Bonn. We were received by Henry Cabot Lodge, the ambassador himself. He insisted that he could only receive a three-man delegation and I was included.

'We had no choice. The Russians would have used your congress as an excuse to march into Czechoslovakia. We are sorry,' he told us.

So was the German government. We got 50,000 Deutsche Marks from an "anonymous" donor after all the noise died down. We put it into a foundation that promoted the cultivation of Latvian heritage among Latvian youth in the West. One of the things we did was to produce a record by a publishing company we dubbed *The KGB*. It featured popular Latvian songs sung by a Latvian actor in Latvia. Some of the songs were banned because the text could be interpreted in a different light to that set by the Party. It so happened that the Russian acronym *KGB* for the Soviet Secret Service Agency (*Komitet Gosudarstvenno Bezopasnosti*) was the same as the name of our publishing company KGB, which in Latvian meant Society for the Preservation of Culture (*Kultūras Glābšanas Biedrība*), newly founded by the Latvian youth living in exile. This album was smuggled into Soviet Latvia and was a great hit.

A much more serious matter was developing in Czechoslovakia than a mere exiled youth congress in Berlin. A month after the Hanover congress Russian tanks rolled in. The Czech Communist party leader, Alexander Dubček was aiming to reform communism and introduce "socialism with a human face" into his country. But it was not just the Russian tanks that stopped him. All the communist "allies"; Poland, East Germany, Bulgaria, Rumania and Hungary contributed with their share of tanks to defeat the peaceful Czech revolt. The "allies" had no choice, otherwise they would have suffered the same fate as Czechoslovakia. Poor Hungary had its own uprising crushed by Soviet tanks in a bloody war in 1956. I remember a young Hungarian refugee who arrived at Heidelberg Junior Technical School, where I was enrolled after I'd completed my primary school education at Greensborough. He looked just like the Latvians who'd arrived six years earlier from the camps in Germany. His hair style, clothes, his whole appearance said Europe, east of the Berlin Wall.

I arrived in Stockholm after the Hanover congress mostly by bumming rides from one country to another on my European "tour". I immediately landed in the middle of a huge demonstration. Police wearing helmets and mounted on big horses were protecting the Soviet embassy. With thousands of others behind me I stood in the front line and protested the Soviet crushing of the reform movement in Czechoslovakia. By now we had heard through the underground grapevine in Latvia of the tragic death of a Latvian officer in Prague. National units in the Red Army had long been abolished and everybody had to serve in the one, Soviet army, which, in effect was Russian. The officer was a tank commander. He had walked into a pub and all the Czechs got up and jeered at him. He shouted that he was not a Russian, pulled out his revolver, and shot himself.

In 1970 I couldn't believe I ended up in Rīga. Actually, I was back in Rīga, though I couldn't remember a thing of my life in Latvia before my family fled to the West. It was summertime and the weather was quite hot and humid. I think the summer of 1944 was also very hot. I was a guest of the KGB, well, not quite. I was a guest of the *Committee for Cultural Exchange with Countrymen Overseas*, which was a front for the KGB. But it was politically incorrect to say that, so everybody was all smiles and all ears, listening politely to the recitations of Latvian cultural achievements in all spheres of life, while under Russian occupation. Latvia no longer existed on the map, other than as a socialist republic of the Soviet Union, but I had to see the country of my parents and where I was born to see if it really existed. Was there a country in the world where people spoke Latvian in the shops and the streets?

I did find out. At first I only heard the Russian language spoken, except at the Cultural Committee of course, and all the events they arranged with the local Latvians. The unspoken rule for speaking Latvian was as follows: unless you knew the other person or persons, you first spoke in Russian, then switched to Latvian, when it was mutually recognized that both sides were Latvian. The same procedure was repeated in shops. It was different in the countryside, where Latvians were still in the majority. Latvian theatres were the last refuge of true Latvian language and culture. Though there were still Latvian schools, the Russian schools were gaining the upper hand as more and more Russian immigrants arrived. The living standard in Latvia was still much higher than it was in Russia. All the minority schools for Poles, Lithuanians, Jews and Germans that existed during the period of Latvia's independence had been abolished. Latvia was fast becoming a Russian province where some privileges were still granted to the aborigines.

The wonderful world of communism was fast approaching and it was becoming increasingly evident that everybody, irrespective of nationality, would soon speak the "rich and versatile" Russian language because it was more practical and progressive. So how did communist Russia differ from tsarist Russia? In substance it was the same Russification program, only the outward appearance had changed.

I was crushed. In addition to coming to terms with the reality of the situation I had to make contact with the underground. I had my first scare when I was crossing the Finnish-Russian border by train at Viborg, a town that Russia seized from Finland during the Second World War.

'Do you have any literature?' the Russian border guard asked me in fairly good English.

'No,' I replied.

He groped my jacket that was hanging by the window and must have felt the newspaper I had stuffed in the inside pocket. My heart missed a beat but he didn't say anything. The newspaper was printed in Stockholm and was the organ of the Latvian Social Democrats, the so-called *Mensheviks* in communist terminology, the greatest sinners of all, who had betrayed the noble communist cause and joined the "bourgeoisie camp". I had cleared my first hurdle.

Imants Lešinskis was my handler in Rīga. He was a pleasant enough fellow to talk to. He was the chairman of the Cultural Committee and had organized a week's intensive "short course" in proper Soviet thinking for me. I got the red carpet treatment. We wined and dined at the best restaurants which were only open to the cream of communist society, or those with *blat*, some goods or service you could offer that couldn't be obtained elsewhere in a society of pronounced scarcity. He was intelligent, ready to concede a point, showed flexibility in interpreting history and politely fended off my questions and accusations with down-to-earth "reality checks".

'What is the alternative to the present political model Latvians live in?' Imants countered. 'Yes, we have had a rotten history of the big powers trampling all over us, but, Atis, Moscow would be crazy to put an end to the Latvian people - they are the best workers in the Soviet Union! Look at the wealth Latvia is producing!'

Was it wise to submit myself to this subtle brain-washing, I wondered? But this was the indoctrination fed to Latvians here from the cradle to the grave and I couldn't make myself an exception if I was to understand the system and my people.

'Atis,' Imants continued, 'there are not many of us. Politics isn't going to change anything. You saw what happened in Berlin. We all want the Latvian youth in the West to keep their ties with the home country. The best way is for them to see first-hand the cultural achievements of the Latvian nation, and one way to do that is for our young poets, writers, artists and scientists to come and visit you in Europe and America and thus keep the bond alive with the generation growing up in Latvia. Otherwise all the young Latvians in the West will be lost to the Latvian people. They will lose the language because they are growing up in isolation from the main nation.'

I remembered what an American professor of war studies had told me when I asked him what I could do to free my country.

'Atis, how many Latvians are there?' he asked.

'Not quite one and a half million. We lost a third of our population during and after the war. But we have over two million if you include the Russian settlers.'

'Well, we could put that many people in our Ford factories.'

From that I was to understand that we were too small to warrant global attention.

After knocking on the doors of half the UN delegation offices in New York, I received at best only a sympathetic hearing when I proposed a vote demanding independence for all three Baltic States. Nobody was even ready to talk about giving the Baltic States a sort of half-way independence status, like that of the communist Warsaw Pact states of Poland or Czechoslovakia. It seemed to me that except for the rhetoric, nobody was interested in lifting even a finger to help the Baltic States regain their independence.

I failed to convince Imants Lešinskis that for my study of the 1905 revolution in Latvia, which I gave as the ostensible purpose for my visit, I would also need to interview a former revolutionary and social democrat and not just take notes from documents and books in the libraries. He said he would think it over. After a few days, during a sumptuous dinner in one of the "select" restaurants called *Pūt vējiņi* (Blow little wind) in Rīga's Old Town, he slowly lowered his wine glass and peered over the rim of his glasses as he was want to do when he wanted to make a point.

'That interview, Atis, I'm afraid that we will not be able to arrange it.' Was it the local Latvian KGB "boys" or the KGB Center in Moscow who had seen through my ploy, I wondered. The person I wanted to interview was my underground man. I was checkmated. Well, almost. I gave my copy of the Latvian Social Democrats newspaper to somebody else I knew I could trust. I was taken aback by the effect it had on him. He took it and read it from the first page to the last. I ceased to exist until he had read every last word!

Back at the hotel I heard a knock on my door. I opened it and a man some ten years older than me entered.

'I am Paulis Irbe's son, Imants. Paulis is your mother, Anna's, brother.'
'You are my cousin, then? I asked.
'That's right. Let's go to Jūrmala and meet your uncle.'

My Uncle Paulis was delighted to see me but seemed a little cautious about what he said.

'Just last month a whole village from Russia was settled here,' he exclaimed after some time. 'We are becoming strangers in our own land.'
I noticed he said this when Imants was not in the room.

When the plane landed in Stockholm from Helsinki I dropped to my knees and kissed the ground - I was out of prison! But it took me some months to overcome the habit of furtively glancing over my shoulder to check if I was being followed. I continued to reflect on my meetings with Imants Lešinskis - was he O'Brien, the Thought Police officer or Charrington, the amiable antique-shop dealer, in George Orwell's book, *1984?* How high up was he?

While in Rīga I had kept a little diary, which I always carried with me. My hotel room was searched daily. I rewrote my "shorthand" into a little primer about "soft" Soviet indoctrination. In 1976 this book was published in the Latvian language in Stockholm; earlier it had been run in the biggest Latvian exile newspaper, *Laiks* in New York. I called it *Gorkija iela 11a* (Gorky Street 11a), which was the address of the Cultural Committee in Rīga. It caused a sensation, I had exposed the Cultural Committee as a KGB organization and the mode of thinking of its top policy planners. The KGB was of another opinion, and banished me from visiting Latvia forever. No more visas would be granted to me.

I had moved to Sweden, to be closer to Latvia. One morning I was awoken by a phone call from a friend.

'Atis, guess what? Imants Lešinskis has jumped ship! He's with the Americans now.'

The news hit me like a bomb had exploded in my apartment. That my old mentor, Imants Lešinskis would betray the KGB and join up with the CIA - well - I was speechless. Lešinskis had worked his way up the KGB ladder and was eventually entrusted to a top position in the United Nations in New York as a covert KGB agent. The UN paid his wages, half of which he transferred back to the KGB. But one fine day he and his wife and daughter stepped into a taxi with a heavy suitcase and defected to the USA.

I couldn't wait to talk to him! When he visited Stockholm he was surrounded by droves of Swedish secret police. No doubt he had lots to tell them. He also had a lot to say to Dr. Bruno Kalniņš, the head of the Latvian social democrats in exile, the same chap whom my mother had regretted not seeing speak at a political rally all those years ago. He also talked at length with Dr. Uldis Ģērmanis, the eminent Latvian historian. Kalniņš and Ģērmanis were the two main Latvian targets of Soviet propaganda who were living in the West.[17] Lešinskis thanked me for giving him top marks in my primer, *Gorkija iela 11a*. Thanks to my description of him as the only one with a brain in the whole Soviet

---

17 For an excellent book on Latvian history, that is a real page turner, see *The Latvian Saga* by Uldis Ģērmanis, Rīga, Atēnas Publishing House, 2008. Another excellent book about the three Baltic States is *A History of the Baltic States* by Andres Kasekamp, New York, Palgrave/Macmillan, 2010.

Latvian propaganda apparatus he was promoted to colonel in the KGB ranks and was eventually transferred to spy on the UN.

He told me I had been too hard a nut to crack. Others had been easier. I wondered what would have happened if I had been persuaded by him to mold the political program of the Second World Latvian Youth congress (this time held in London) away from an independent Latvian platform to that of a neutral one. He had been careful not to ask for a pro-Soviet agenda, as he knew this would have been rejected. But a neutral program for the sake of seeing famous poets and artists from Latvia was a realistic possibility, especially because this approach was pushed very hard by a group of exiled youth calling themselves the *New Left*, which had strong contacts, yes, with the Cultural Committee in Rīga, headed by the mastermind, Imants Lešinskis.

I felt a chill run down my spine. I had corresponded with Lešinskis for nigh on two years about the possibility of inviting cultural speakers from Latvia to the London youth congress. I was still living in California then. Surely the FBI must have gone through our mail. It could not have been otherwise. I must have come under suspicion. The FBI had no idea I was playing a game with Lešinskis to draw out enough information from him to justify rejecting his proposal of a politically neutral congress. Then I could deflect responsibility onto him and away from myself for not inviting the Latvian cultural personalities to the London congress. I succeeded and our political struggle for freedom was not compromised but I knew by now there must be a fat FBI file on me. I wondered who the Latvian was in the USA who translated my letters. Imants Lešinskis died in a Washington car park not long after our meeting in Stockholm. It was reported he'd had a heart attack. Perhaps. From the time I knew him in Rīga he drank heavily and smoked three packets of cigarettes a day.

During the Christmas of 1979, the TV and radios were blaring out the news that Soviet paratroopers had stormed the Afghan presidential palace and tanks had rolled into the capital, Kabul. The Soviet occupation of

Afghanistan had begun. I couldn't sleep. Once more Latvian soldiers would have to fight and die in a foreign army, an army that had occupied their land and was now occupying another. Would it ever end?

Then I began to wonder, was there anything I could do to put a stop to it? But how? Could I find a Latvian, Estonian or Lithuanian prisoner of war who was being held by the Afghan resistance and take him to the West, to America? If the Baltic soldiers started deserting from the Soviet army in great numbers, and then ended up in the West, would Moscow stop sending them to Afghanistan? But to do that I would have to put my own body on the line and go to war! For three nights I felt a yellow streak developing up my spine. It was awful. It made me sick. Then it disappeared. I was free to go and started sleeping soundly again. But I had no money. And I had torn a muscle in my leg running up a hill while training.

I became the Latvian representative on the executive committee organizing the International Afghanistan Tribunal, run by the Swedes, which would judge the Soviet occupation of Afghanistan and decide whether they were committing atrocities against civilians. It turned out that many of these particular Swedes belonged to the Chinese communist camp - so - like Mao they did not recognize the occupation of the Baltic States! I was elected to the executive committee as a representative of an independent Latvia, not an exiled organization. At the tribunal I made contact with the Afghan commanders who were fighting against the Soviet army and explained to them the Baltic situation. They were very friendly and were ready to offer their help.

The Soviet Union was getting into more trouble. A second front was opening up in Europe against Moscow. The Poles were sticking their heads up. They had a huge organization called *Solidarity* and a trade union leader named Lech Walensa. Poland was a much bigger country than Czechoslovakia or Hungary. It had quite a big army. The Soviets were sure to get a beating if they rolled into Warsaw with their tanks. I was working at the Swedish Institute of International Affairs and had time to read the journals devoted to international security. Some western security experts were beginning to make the case that complete Soviet hegemony of central Europe was no longer sustainable and should be reviewed. They were advancing ideas about a "Finlandization" of that part of Europe whereby the communist countries would become more independent and democratic but still by some kind of political formula observe the "legitimate security interests" of the Soviet Union. But the Baltic States were not in the picture. Why not include them in the "Finlandization" project, I asked myself.

The Baltic youth living in exile were also becoming more assertive. I was involved in their activities even though I wasn't so young any more. We chartered a ship called the *Baltic Star* and planned to steam past the Baltic coast and then dock in Helsinki. Finland was hosting a conference to mark the 10th anniversary of the *Conference on European Security and Cooperation*. Once again, American, Canadian and European heads of state and the Soviet Union were going to assemble in Helsinki to hold speeches and congratulate one another. We planned to arrive a few days earlier, when the world's media would be waiting for the big guys to arrive and remind them about the Baltic States. It was our reply to Berlin. Thanks to the heavy handed attempts of the Soviet propaganda machine we got all the coverage we needed even before we left Stockholm harbor. Moscow called us CIA agents and every media reporter in Stockholm worth their salt rushed to see what three hundred CIA agents looked like! A bomb scare was concocted to stop us from boarding but after the ritual police search by the dog squad, we were allowed to set sail amid much fanfare.

We slowly slid passed the Latvian town of Ventspils where my parents had met and lived for a while. If I squinted I could make out the huge, silvery oil tanks shimmering in the noon day heat. It was a major Latvian oil terminal for the Soviet Union but we were safe as we kept just inside international waters, a bare 12 kilometers from the coastline.

We continued on to Finland and marched through the streets of Helsinki. The Finns were surprised to see the three Baltic flags after a 45 year absence and applauded us, some even joined us. Vladimir Bukovski, a leading Russian dissident writer living in exile in London, gave a heartfelt speech about freedom at the end of the parade.

After the ship returned to Stockholm we held the first *Baltic Futures Seminar*. The foreign experts were careful to speak only about their areas of interest. It may have been different if Professor Zbigniev Brzezinski had come. He wrote to me to say he couldn't make it this time but would next time. He was the former national security advisor to US President Jimmy Carter, who had stood at the Khyber Pass with a rifle in his hands after the Soviets marched into Afghanistan. I offered the "Finlandization" plan for central Europe - what arguments were there for not including the Baltics in that project? Weren't the Baltic States a litmus test for Western relations with the Soviet Union? Did the West mean what it said about not recognizing the Baltic States as being part of the USSR? The papers were printed later in the *Journal of Baltic Studies* published by the Association for the Advancement of Baltic Studies. It was the beginning of the internationalization of the Baltic security debate, I told myself. The experts couldn't ignore the Baltic States anymore.

In the heat of summer in 1986 after climbing a steep hill I saw that the border post between Pakistan and Afghanistan was in ruins.

'No visas necessary?' I asked my new Afghan friends.

'Gun is visa,' they laughed.

Then a deafening bang went off to our left followed immediately by a tremendous rush of air above our heads. We had been spotted by the Afghan Communist Army garrison several kilometers away. I had almost been lifted up off the ground by the back draft caused by the shell as it screamed over our heads. One of the Afghans clutched my hand, shielding my side from the direction the shells were coming from, then led me at a smart pace across the wide, rock-strewn, dry river bed.

'Special greeting for you Atis,' the Afghan joked as we waited for the others to catch up.

The assault on the mujahedin started two days later in Surhab canyon. I was awoken in the cave where we were spending the night and told bombs were being dropped. I rushed outside and saw jets streaking in against the mountain we had left the day before and releasing bombs that fell in clusters and then exploded in rapid succession against the hilltop. Some of the mujahedin were trying to shoot the jets down with their RPG 7 anti-tank rocket launchers, a thankless task. The grenades exploded in little puffs of black smoke way behind the fast jets. Soon the tanks would come. It was decided that I would be spirited away to a safe place before the tanks encircled the area. The day before, when we had been trudging through the canyon we passed hundreds of Afghan fighters with their horses, mules and donkeys. I felt a sickening fear mounting inside me as the jets circled above us. I learned this was the first stage in overcoming your fear. You become nervous and don't take things in your stride. For one thing, you don't understand that these planes are only reconnoitering the area.

The second stage is the other extreme - you become rash. This is the most dangerous phase. I remember Uncle Vincis telling me about his experiences on the front, that the first soldiers to get killed were the raw recruits who, lacking patience, recklessly charged up the hill to get at the enemy. I was sitting out in the open trying to take snapshots of the action in the air. The mujahedin signaled for me to come down into the bushes. The third and final stage is when you have adjusted yourself to the nature of war and keep your wits about you. From then on it is only a matter of sound judgment and endurance.

I began to forge new plans after my second trip to Afghanistan. I couldn't find any Baltic soldiers because the fighting always erupted wherever I went. I decided to go all the way - to walk into the Soviet Union itself. My plan was to cross the Amu Darya River that marks the border between Afghanistan and the USSR and poke a finger in Brezhnev's eye. There is a Latvian saying; *If you are thrown out the door you can always climb back in through the window*. I planned to accompany a convoy of arms across Afghanistan and then cross into Soviet Tadjikistan with a party of guerrillas to remind the Politburo that attacking a country need not remain a one way street. But it was not to be. I took a different trip just before we crossed into Afghanistan from Pakistan.

For a fleeting moment I feel better, but then the nausea overtakes me again. What I need now is some fresh air and then things simply must get better! I lurch out of the smelly outhouse and lean against the mud and stone wall encircling the compound gulping fresh air – the air was beginning to cool somewhat – and while waiting for the first signs of improvement, I manage to take note that the two mujahedin on the veranda are eying me strangely.

But that doesn't matter, not in the least bit. I forget them immediately as I soar through the universe of a million stars at a speed that was so fantastic it was incomprehensible to even begin to understand how fast it was. Absolute joy, never before experienced – I was traveling at the speed of light! Where to? Ah – I saw it! There in the distance past the maze of stars more brilliant than diamonds was something gently black and soft, smooth and velvety, radiating a peace so absolute that I can't wait to get there and I try to increase the velocity of my flight. It seems as if I have managed to achieve this miracle, but then a hindrance occurs, which begins to disturb me. At first it's only an annoyance, to be shrugged off since nothing can stop me now from reaching the perfect happiness, but soon I am obliged to acknowledge that it persists and, furthermore, is growing into more than just an annoyance – it is developing into a threat that could jeopardize my amazing flight. In desperation I summon all my strength and put up a fierce struggle to escape it, shake it off, it seems that some horror is clutching at my body and pulling me back. What is it? I have to see it, so I can get rid of it![18]

---

18   For full text see www.lejins.lv, Afganu kalns/Afghan mountain, published 2010-09-25. For a 20 minute documentary of my trips to Afghanistan, made in Stockholm in 1987, see the same website www.lejins.lv/2010/08/18/ar-partizaniem-afganistana/

The mujahedin managed to shake me out of my unconsciousness. They were the "horror". They saved me. I was very, very sick and had to be rushed back down the mountain to the border town of Peshawar. Driving up the mountain the previous day the grapes we bought at the roadside were indeed well washed in the gushing spring water from the side of the mountain but I had forgotten to wash my hands. I almost died from food poisoning. Perhaps my "clinical death" saved me from actual death, had I crossed the Amu Darya river. I sometimes wonder whether there is a deeper meaning to the word *Fate* that has escaped me.

When I returned to Sweden I took a walk in the countryside outside Stockholm with my young son, Ilmārs and a friend from Latvia. A plane flew overhead. I grabbed my son and in less than a second we were both underneath a tree. My friend stared at me, as did my son. The war in Afghanistan had caused me to develop conditioned reflexes, similar to the ones I developed when I had the KGB trailing me in Rīga. Even when I returned to California I inadvertently kept glancing over my shoulder for the first few months until I became aware of it and put a stop to it.

In March 1989 I was standing on a platform at Helsinki railway station waiting for the train from Finland station in Leningrad. I was there to meet the leaders of the Latvian Popular Front and take them by boat to Stockholm. The group was headed by a young man, around thirty years old with a big shock of ash colored hair and intense blue eyes. The ancient Latvians must have looked like him when the German Teutonic Order came up the Daugava River in their boats early in the 12th century.

I had been there at the same place nineteen years before when I climbed onto a train that took me to the Finland station in Leningrad and then onto Rīga. Again I thought back to one of the history books I'd read on the Russian revolution when I was at UCLA. It was called *To the Finland Station* by Edmund Wilson and explained how the German High Command let Lenin and his cohorts travel through Germany in a sealed train from Switzerland to Finland. Lenin must have stepped from this very platform onto a train that took him to the Russian capital,

St. Petersburg, which Leningrad was then called. He must have also stepped out at the Finland station in St. Petersburg in April 1917 and turned the democratic revolution against the Tsar into a communist one. The Russian army collapsed and Germany won the war on the Eastern front, for a while anyway.

I wondered how the West would react to Gorbachev's attempts to reform communism. He was trying to do what poor Alexander Dubček tried to do in Czechoslovakia in 1968. Was it simply a question of better late than never? But Gorbachev was reaching out to the West and both Ronald Reagan and Great Britain's Iron Lady, Margaret Thatcher had discovered that, "You can do business with Gorbachev". Would this business overshadow the Baltic strive for renewed independence?

But first I had to find out where the Latvian Popular Front leaders stood on Latvian independence. Outwardly they were still talking Gorbachev talk on reform of the system and how Lenin's true teachings, perverted by Stalin, must be implemented.

We sat with jugs of beer before us. I hesitated before speaking.
    'What about independence?' I finally asked.
They could hardly wait to answer. They were expecting me to ask all along.
    'Of course we are for re-establishing the Latvian State, but we cannot run ahead of events. We must gather our strength while the political situation matures. Then we will strike.'

They made their case to the Swedish government and political parties. Later the Swedes checked with the Grand Old Man of Baltic politics, Dr. Bruno Kalniņš. He rang me and said to meet him at the palace of the Swedish Foreign Ministry. He had been summoned by the Foreign Minister, Sten Anderson. The minister's room was spacious, quiet and furnished in the style of a bygone era with lots of brass and dark red as the dominant color. You could feel the history in the room. By now I was the head of the Swedish branch of the Popular Front.

'Will the Latvian Popular Front go all the way?' the minister asked.
'Once the Latvian Riflemen start marching, there will be no stopping them. Our young people are their heirs,' Kalniņš replied.

We set up Baltic information offices in Stockholm funded by the Swedish authorities and I became the senior executive officer of the Latvian Information Office, our future embassy. A group of Latvian Popular Front electoral officials arrived - the Swedish trade unions taught them how to win elections. We did win! Even under the Soviet system and with the Soviet army in Latvia voting against the Popular Front's candidates. Barely, but it was enough to prepare the ground through the Soviet legal system to re-establish independence when the opportunity presented itself.

I finally got a visa to visit Latvia again from the Soviet embassy in Stockholm. The Swedish Institute of International Affairs, where I was working as a research assistant had decided to send me a year earlier, in August 1988, on assignment to the Baltic States to write the first on-the-spot report about what was happening there for the institute's monthly "IS." (International Studies). At first I was refused a visa by the Soviet embassy. Thereupon the Swedish institute protested on my behalf to the Soviet Ambassador in Stockholm and he, on instructions from Moscow, arranged a visa for me. The institute had recently concluded a cooperation agreement with the Academy of Science in Moscow and this factor must have swayed the KGB in Moscow to overrule the Latvian communists and the KGB in Rīga who had never forgiven me for writing my primer, *Gorky Street 11a*.

But my trip back to Latvia was not without high drama. On my first day in Rīga I was filming a group of Latvians at a picket line, protesting against the Soviet authorities, when the militia (Soviet police) suddenly surrounded the group and hauled us all off to jail. I was put behind bars along with the Latvians who had been supporting the picket. One fierce policeman dressed in civilian clothes, threatened to "teach me how to speak Russian in five minutes" if I didn't stop talking to him in

Latvian. My fellow Latvians advised me to inform the police that I was an American citizen, and therefore could not be detained for more than twenty minutes. I did so, but the police didn't believe me. However, one policewoman, a Latvian, began to have doubts and must have made enquiries.

I was eventually released but after I called the American consulate in Leningrad to inform them what happened to me, the telephone in my hotel room went dead. It was dead the whole week I was there, but kept ringing at three or four in the morning, waking me up. I was tailed wherever I went, sometimes quite openly. Strangely enough the Rīga Prosecutor summoned me soon afterwards and indirectly apologized for my treatment and detention by the police. The American embassy must have made formal enquiries in Moscow and the local Soviet authorities in Rīga must have been told to behave themselves by the bosses in Moscow.

On 19th of August, 1991 I was driving through the pleasant Latvian countryside from Vecpiebalga in central Latvia back to Rīga with some friends. We stopped at the local store. Everybody around us was strangely silent. The Soviet army had taken Rīga! The Soviet reactionaries had launched a *coup d'état* in Moscow against Gorbachev and declared a state of emergency! Gorbachev disappeared and was said to be under house arrest, but we couldn't work out if he was with the reactionaries or against them. He may have become frightened of his own reform efforts and clandestinely sided with the coup leaders because the very existence of the Soviet Union was now being threatened. Boris Yeltsin had emerged as the leader of the Russian democratic forces and seized the initiative against the Soviet coup leaders. We knew who he was. He had been to Rīga and plotted with the Latvian Popular Front against Gorbachev, who would not let the Baltics go. He had jumped onto the top of a tank in Moscow and called on the Russian people not to obey the coup leaders. What would the army do? Would it back Yeltsin and a free Russia against the counter-revolution?

We hurried back to my friend's country house and turned on the TV. We saw the familiar face of the female Latvian announcer warning the people of Latvia that the broadcast would soon stop - soldiers were already rushing up the stairs. Then the screen went blank. The Popular Front had made preparations in case there was a counter-revolution and had called this the X hour. Therefore we knew what to do and tuned into the underground radio. Though the signal was weak, we could hear it. Strangely enough foreign TV continued to be transmitted for a while. We saw the President of France, Francoise Mitterand congratulate the coup organizers and extend his recognition to them. Was that the end of reform in the Soviet Union and the reestablishment of Baltic independence?

I slept with an axe next to me at night. I would not be taken like my Uncle Vitauts - led out of his house like a sheep. I would take at least two of them with me into the next world.

The next day we returned to Rīga. The traffic slowed as we reached the gates of Rīga. We saw tanks circling the city, the soldiers were from central Asia but the officers were Russian. They peered at us as we drove by. We looked straight ahead.

I scouted around for a long time before I snuck inside my apartment. Someone had left a message for me with my landlady. She told me there was going to be an emergency meeting of the Popular Front board and the address where it was going to be held. The underground grapevine was working.

The TV stations began broadcasting again. They were now in the hands of the counter-revolutionaries. It showed Alfreds Rubiks, the leader of the Latvian communists, warning the Latvian people that if they resisted the seizure of power by the coup leaders dire consequences would follow. We knew that he was one of the few communists who was a true believer. He stuck with the Party when most Latvians deserted it.

Rubiks was convinced that Uncle Stalin had brought freedom, milk and honey to the Latvian people in 1940.

Fearing an attack, my friends and I left the Popular Front headquarters in a hurry and barricaded ourselves inside the stately parliament building along with the members of the Popular Front government. The building was surrounded by a makeshift wall of cement blocks and huge rocks. It was originally built by the Baltic German nobility in the 19th century as their seat of power during the tsarist reign in Latvia. Even after Peter the Great conquered the Baltics from Sweden the local German nobility ruled locally through a Baltic autonomy agreement with imperial Russia.

After Latvia gained independence in the War of National Liberation in 1918 -1920, the building became the Latvian parliament, called the *Saeima*. (Dear reader, please note that "little" Latvia defeated both Germany and Russia in the War of National Liberation, partly by playing one big power off against the other. This same scenario however, did not play out so well during the Second World War.) From 1940 the building housed the puppet Soviet Latvian parliament, called the Supreme Soviet. Now it was controlled by the Popular Front! We all had but one thought - would this building once again become the house of parliament of a free Latvia?

The *Omon*, nick-named the black berets, the special Soviet Ministry of Interior troops, were rampaging outside, throwing canisters of tear gas and trying to pull down the barricades the people had set up around the parliamentary building. The Popular Front Government leader, Ivars Godmanis was sweating inside with his bodyguards, who were clutching their little automatic pistols that looked like plastic toys. He looked sallow as he gave me a smile.

'Atis, how does this compare to Afghanistan?' he asked.

'Actually,' I replied, 'I felt safer there. We were much better armed.'

All of a sudden the *Omon* troops jumped into their armored vehicles and roared off. An eerie silence descended on Old Town Rīga. The gas clouds dispersed like morning fog. Then the news broke - the coup had failed in Moscow! Now was the time to act! The Popular Front deputies hurriedly voted for the restoration of independence of Latvia! I sat in the great hall of the *Saeima* and held my breath - how would the elected representatives of the people vote? In the same hall, fifty-one years previously, the "elected" deputies voted unanimously for the incorporation of Latvia into the paradise of nations called the Soviet Union under the "benevolent" leadership of Comrade Stalin. Back then not one single deputy dared to vote against incorporation, not even to abstain.

I could breathe again. Restoration was a fact, but only just! It was 21st August 1991. After much drama a two-thirds majority was gained. There was plenty of opposition. It came from the so-called *Interfront,* the pro-Soviet faction, most of whom could not give their speeches in the Latvian language because they held it in such disdain and therefore had refused to learn how to speak it during the occupation. As members of the rapidly growing Russian community, they were part of the on-going Russification program. Independence was achieved despite the presence of the Russian army which had some 200,000 soldiers still stationed in Latvia!

Yeltsin, who was now the leader of Russia, recognized Baltic independence - after which the Western countries, except Iceland, followed. Iceland didn't wait for the green light from Moscow - she recognized Baltic independence before Russia did. There was some furious backpedaling done by some of the Western capital leaders who had jumped the gun in recognizing the coup leaders.

If only Yeltsin had recognized the restoration of independence of the three Baltic countries of Estonia, Latvia and Lithuania and not just recognized their independence! They were not suddenly newly emerging countries coming out of the collapsing Soviet empire like Belarus, Ukraine or the central Asian republics. What a difference one word can make! The Baltic States were independent before 1940. If Russia could not come to terms with her past, wasn't she bound to repeat it with a new generation who had not learned the lessons of the past? Wouldn't she eventually start pawing at us again?

The next day I was in the crowd watching the security forces of free Latvia, called the White Berets, and the pro-Latvian militia, soon to become the police, take over the KGB building. We all rushed to the imposing building of the Communist Party's Central Committee. There was black smoke coming from the windows. They were burning documents. The White Berets brought out Alfred Rubiks in handcuffs. I knew some of the security guys. They were veterans of the Afghan war. 'We found a list drawn up by the coup organizers of two hundred Popular Front people who were to be shot on the spot and a list of four hundred others who were to be deported to concentration camps in Belarus,' one of them whispered to me. Which list was I on, I wondered?

These lists "disappeared" over the next few days. Nobody knew what happened to them. Now we are celebrating I thought to myself, but it could take a generation to clean out the KGB agents, all the moles, who are most certainly going to be left behind after the retreat of the empire. But what if the empire comes back before then?

I walked the cobblestoned streets of Old Town looking for rooms to set up the Latvian Institute of International Affairs. If we'd had such an institute before the Second World War maybe we wouldn't have been caught so unprepared for what was to come after the signing of the Hitler-Stalin pact. At that time the Latvian people didn't even know that most of the Latvian communists living in Russia had been shot by Stalin's men. There was censorship, which also meant that you were not allowed to say anything considered derogatory about our big neighbor to the east. An independent Latvian research institute would have seen the approaching threats a long time before they happened. The Swedish Institute of International Affairs gave me some money and was ready to train researchers as part of their aid program to Latvia.

I entered a building through an open door. There was a Russian soldier standing inside. His jaw dropped as I walked passed him, he hesitated, bewildered I suppose at my behavior. I hadn't asked for permission to enter! I ran up the stairs and pulled open a door. Inside all movement froze as a hundred eyes stared at me in astonishment. The room was full of people hastily packing boxes of index cards and bundles of documents into crates. What was happening here? The colonial administration beating a hasty retreat? Nobody could understand what I was saying. Clearly they couldn't speak a word of Latvian. The uncomfortable silence became oppressive and I made a rapid exit. The guard was staring at the telephone on his desk. It seemed he had nobody to ring to report to. The army was also packing to leave.

Finally I found "the little red room" in the University of Latvia's History and Philosophy Faculty as the home for the new institute. It was the study center for Marxism-Leninism at the faculty. But I administered a jolt alright for both students and teachers when I put a sign on the door with the institute's name written in two languages - Latvian and underneath, in smaller letters, English. All signs up till then had been in Latvian and Russian - in equal sized lettering.

I was so busy with the institute's affairs that I hardly had time to pick up my KGB file. There were big gaps in it, like missing teeth. Absent was mention of my "brainwashing" program at the Cultural Exchange Committee, the Peace and Freedom Cruise, which had been filmed from the inside by a Soviet agent and shown on Soviet Latvian TV as a "flagrant anti-Soviet act", my Afghanistan dossier, and so on. These items had clearly been the responsibility of Moscow and not the local Latvian KGB branch.

Street names were changed back to their original names. Gorky Street was now once again Krišjāņa Valdemāra iela and number 11 now housed the Ministry of Culture. The name of the main thoroughfare in Rīga had been changed five times; *Brīvības* (Freedom), *Lenin, Adolf Hitler*, then *Lenin* again before it regained *Brīvības,* in 1991.

The circle had been completed. I was back, living and working in Latvia, which I left when I was two years old. My brother, Aivars and my sister, Aija have remained in California but our parents now rest next to my eldest sister, Ina and my great grandfather, Jānis. I plant flowers on their common grave in spring, and lay small fir branches on it before the snow comes. This is the place where I will also one day finally come to rest.

While translating the English version of my mother's story, *Dzīvot dzīvu dzīvi* I found out from the Latvian Evangelical Lutheran church that Reverend Irbe and his family were deported to Siberia in 1946. He returned alone in 1957 because he couldn't afford to pay for the train tickets for his whole family. His wife and two sons returned later after he saved up the money for the tickets. After the condemnation of Stalin by the new Soviet leader, Nikita Khrushchev in the mid-fifties, followed by some liberalization of communist rule, the deportees who had survived were allowed to return home. But they had to pay their own fare back; no compensation whatsoever was given to them for the destruction of their lives and property. They were treated like pariahs when they returned. They were labeled "enemies of the people" and many people were afraid to associate with them. Even today, Russia, the legal successor of the Soviet Union, is not ready to compensate the victims of Soviet crimes against humanity, unlike Germany. Instead it is the Latvian State, itself a victim, that has established a special budgetary item to assist the victims of the deportation who are still alive today.

I wrote to Zbigniev Brzezinski in Washington and invited him to my first big international conference on Baltic security held in Rīga, 1993. This was a continuation of the Baltic Futures seminars held in Stockholm. He remembered my first invitation in 1985 and arrived to speak on the controversial issue of NATO enlargement. Carl Bildt, the Swedish prime minister also came, as did Adam Rotfeld, head of the Stockholm International Peace Research Institute, who later became Poland's foreign minister. The Soros Auditorium was packed - even some members of parliament came. That was the beginning. But I have to end my story here because my journey back to Latvia has ended and

I have begun a new journey in Latvia. That's a different story and so I will just press the fast-forward button on the time machine and say that the three Baltic States did join the EU and NATO and, after a brief spell of fantastic economic growth, were knocked backwards in their development by the effects of the global economic crisis of 2008-09.

Latvians are regaining their language and learning to speak Latvian to the so-called "Russian speakers", and these likewise are learning to do the same with the Latvians. But Russia is growing strong again and cannot resist the old imperial impulse to exert her politics onto "near abroad", that is, all the countries that were part of the Soviet Union, even as the shadow of a new world power, China, is steadily growing over the vast empty lands of Siberia my father journeyed through on his return to Latvia.

What is disturbing now is the reintroduction of the Thought Police in Russia whereby secret agents can come to you and affect your behavior if you are planning to do something which they deem inappropriate. You can't act or think freely anymore without fear of repercussions. What this can lead to is described in Arthur Koestler's book, *Darkness at Noon*, first published in 1940. It says on the back cover of my Penguin edition, *"One of the few books written in this epoch which will survive it."* Survive because that epoch is coming back?

I have always had an attachment to London through my parents that began before I was born. The three of us were there in 1970. I had been on the road searching for the Kremlin's Achilles heel so hadn't seen them for two years. They came from Los Angeles to visit my Dad's brother, John and his family in London. Through letters we agreed to rendezvous at the Victoria station.

After that I kept returning to London. Even when I was safely living back in Latvia I took occasional trips to London in my role as director of the Latvian Institute of International Affairs and also when I went to speak to groups of Latvians who had not returned to Latvia since independence was regained. I liked traveling on the underground and reflected how my parents had often taken the same journey so many years before. In 2005 I participated in a conference hosted by the London Institute of International Affairs, which is located in St. James Square, and serviced by the Piccadilly Circus underground station. I traveled between this station and Russell Square on the Piccadilly line, where I was staying in a hotel with my wife, Vita who had joined me so we could do some sightseeing together. Two weeks later, on July 7, we were stunned as we sat watching the news back home in Rīga - four bombs had exploded in London, one of them at "our" - Russell Square - underground station! Altogether 56 people, including the four suicide bombers, were killed and over 700 innocent civilians were injured. Islamic terrorists had struck in the heart of London.

Did Fate step in and save me once again? The terrorists could have struck earlier. Maybe they were going to but something happened to delay their attacks. Likewise in 1945, my parents could have decided to travel through Dresden just one day earlier but they waited and avoided being caught up in the terrible carpet bombing. Is it all just coincidence, I wonder?

In 2009 my son, Ilmārs, who is a major in the Latvian army, went to Afghanistan to command a group of Latvian and American soldiers to train an Afghan battalion high up in the mountains only a few kilometers from the Pakistan border. The Afghan National Army, the American army and the Latvian army have all suffered casualties there. The Latvian and American soldiers who had been training together at the Latvian army base, Ādaži wanted to know what Afghanistan was like before they boarded the plane. I showed them the documentary, *Debt to Afghanistan*[19] produced by Latvian film-maker, Askolds Saulītis.

The documentary is about Latvian soldiers serving in the Soviet Army in Afghanistan during the Soviet occupation between 1979 and 1989 and

---

19 See www.35mm.lv/about filmography/films/36;

Latvian soldiers serving in the Latvian National Army in Afghanistan in response to the September 11 attack on America in 2001.

I'm the film's protagonist with my "Don Quixote" mission to Afghanistan and my reunion in 2005 with the mujahedin commander, Taher Shirzad. He survived the war and persecution by the Taliban. He gave me refuge during the battle for Surhab canyon in 1986. Though his village was controlled by the Afghan communist army I lived in his house for ten days before the fighting died down. There had been two major battles raging on two fronts not far from his village. We observed soviet helicopters flying, as thick as flies, overhead and when the battles died down, I watched from behind the bushes as numerous soviet army tanks and armed personnel carriers passed through the village on their way back to Kabul. As I looked at the soldiers sitting on the tanks I wondered if any of my countrymen were among them. Less than one hundred meters separated us. I felt as if I could stretch out my hand and reach out to them and overcome the bridge that separated us.

My son, Ilmārs returned safely to his wife who was waiting for him with their first child, a son born while he was fighting in Afghanistan.

'Dad, this is enough,' Ilmārs said. 'Edvards, your grandson, will not follow in our footsteps.'

I wonder how long we need to keep repaying our debt to the Afghan people for beating the Soviet Army. The retreat of the Soviet army from Afghanistan did not stop at the Soviet borders. It continued unbroken until the Russian army left Poland, Hungary, Czechoslovakia, Bulgaria, Rumania, East Germany, Latvia, Lithuania, Estonia, Georgia, Azerbaijan, Armenia and all of Central Asia. An empire cannot afford to lose a major war.

Why did things go so badly in Afghanistan after the Soviet army left? The Hollywood film, *Charlie Wilson's War* graphically shows that the USA lost interest in Afghanistan after the Soviets pulled out in 1989. This fits in with my observations. After a decade of destruction and the continued rivalry between Pakistan and India, with each trying to deny the other influence in Afghanistan, the USA made a strategic mistake by turning its back on Afghanistan. In the chaos and civil war that followed the retreat of the Soviet army, the Taliban, aided by Pakistan, came to power. The result was Osama bin Laden and the September 11 attacks on America in 2001. What should happen now, after nine years of fighting the Taliban? Try to bring India and Pakistan together? - their struggle to gain power over one another is the root of the problem. That was already clear to me in 1986 when I saw Indians fighting on the side of the Soviets only because Pakistan was aiding the Afghan freedom fighters.

I'm back in Greensborough, Australia swinging on that willow branch and, while looking at the setting sun, I clearly see my future. Through my mother's eyes I can go back in time and see the first part of the century, before I was born. But there is one flight in time I still cannot take - that is - the next ten to fifteen years when I am going to make Latvia a superpower in alternative energy. This will not be easy - both powerful domestic and foreign interests are opposed to the idea. They want to keep Latvia totally dependent on Russian gas even though she has all the means and possible opportunities to become a leader in the generation of biomass energy. With her vast forests and open spaces she could grow even more energy. Latvia is now the eighth cleanest country on the planet.

In October 2010 I was elected as a member of the Latvian parliament, the Saeima. This should be a good start to my plan as I can influence legislation towards my goal. I will not be alone, other members have similar views.

I have to make a confession. In that willow tree I made a pledge to bring down the Soviet Union. Well, that worked out quite well. Will my next assignment be as successful? I don't know - but I do know it will be my final battle.

Atis in Afghanistan 1987 with commander Fakir

Soviet special forces OMON rampaging in Riga August 21, 1991

28831246R00113

Made in the USA
Lexington, KY
03 January 2014